19093

JEANE DIXON:

The Witnesses

Denis Brian

JEANE DIXON:
The Witnesses

1976
Doubleday & Company, Inc., Garden City, New York

The author wishes to acknowledge, with thanks, the following for permission to reproduce previously published material: the American Society for Psychical Research and Dr. Gardner Murphy, whose paper, "Direct Contacts with Past and Future: Retrocognition and Precognition," was printed in the January 1967 issue of the *Journal of the ASPR*, pp. 8–9; *Parade* magazine; the New York *Times* for the extract from "Dixonmania" by Marcia Seligsen © 1969 by the New York Times Company, reprinted by permission; Time Inc., for permission to reproduce extracts from "$3,000,000 Sham" by David Nevin which appeared in *Life* magazine © 1967 Time Inc. The author also wishes to thank, for their help and co-operation, *The National Enquirer* and *The National Observer*.

Library of Congress Cataloging in Publication Data
Brian, Denis.
Jean Dixon: the witnesses.
Bibliography: p. 213
1. Prophecies (Occult sciences)   2. Dixon, Jeane.
BF1815.D57B74   133.3'092'4
ISBN 0-385-11243-2
Library of Congress Catalog Card Number 75–21212

To Martine with love

ACKNOWLEDGMENTS

My thanks for their help, advice and encouragement, to Laura A. Dale, Dr. Gardner Murphy, Dr. J. B. Rhine, Dr. Louisa E. Rhine, Dr. Edgar Mitchell, and, of course, Jeane Dixon.

FOREWORD BY JEANE DIXON

I was shocked when I began to read this book—shocked as you are when you first hear your own voice on tape. Shocked and bitterly disappointed.

I'll tell you why.

It has always been a practice of mine on a trip, when I arrive at my destination, to turn to the Bible, open it at random, and whatever is on that page is my lesson for the day. Sometimes other books come my way and in them I find my message.

So it was when I read the manuscript of *Jeane Dixon: The Witnesses.* I opened it at random and began to read. It was like touching a live electric wire. Another slanted book! Another attempt to deny the truth and give publicity to lies, half truths, and innuendoes.

But as I read more, starting this time from the beginning, I realized that the author had been true to his intentions—to present the facts, and the facts of course include what my critics have said about me as well as the testimony of my supporters. He has given everyone a chance to be heard—and what more could you ask when the aim is to get as close to the facts as is humanly possible?

Writers often set out to debunk me and the whole field of ESP.

And they search only for the evidence that will bolster their argument. I remember when Jess Stearn came to see me and had dinner with me, he was going to debunk everything about ESP, and me along with it. And when I was able to tell him things he knew I had no normal way of knowing, and when he interviewed people who knew me and also saw me on NBC accurately predicting Sputnik would be orbited—then he knew there was something to it.

The famous psychologist and philosopher William James said there was among many people "a will to believe"; that they are only too ready to accept mysteries and miracles as facts. There is also "a will to disbelieve," and "a will to deceive." But fortunately, in time, the truth prevails.

Several years ago Denis Brian began asking me questions about my ability to predict accurately, and the questioning has gone on over the years. I found him to be searching, informed—and persistent. He has never misquoted me—and retains an open-minded approach, the mark of all effective investigators.

There are of course many questions I can't answer. I don't know why, for example, President Franklin Roosevelt's doctor, Vice-Admiral Ross McIntire, hid from him the fact that the President was a very sick man, that a stroke or fatal heart attack could occur at any time—and this shortly before he was contemplating his fourth term. FDR behaved mysteriously, too, avoiding asking his doctors even the most cursory questions about his own health or life expectancy.

But President Roosevelt twice called me to the White House, and when he asked me how much longer he had to complete his work I told him he had only a short time left. How strange that he would ignore the wealth of medical advice at his command and call me to tell him! Jim Bishop reveals this conspiracy of silence over FDR's health in his book *FDR's Last Year*—but fails to mention my two visits to the White House.

The Secret Service, the National Archives, the Roosevelt Library have no record of my visits, so that officially and in the history books there is no mention of them. How much is lost to history, I wonder, because it isn't in the records.

But it happened. And Denis Brian's attempts to find one irrefutable witness to confirm my White House visits, racing against time as he approaches the book's publishing deadline, read like an exciting detective story. Did he find the witness? And who was it? You'll have to read that for yourself.

When asked to explain my gift for seeing the future, I tell my questioners I could no more explain it than I could really define love or electricity. And when asked to explain why I am a prophet only of doom, I say this is not so. I make many predictions of happy events for people—but these don't make headlines. There are some in this book.

When asked what I believe is our purpose here on earth, I say something like this:

I believe man consists of a body, soul, and Holy Spirit. And through that spirit, God achieves his purpose—which is for us to evolve on the upper spiral of human and spiritual progress.

And to fulfill that purpose the spirit may be reincarnated in many bodies.

The soul, which is uniquely ours—and is not reincarnated—I believe to be the interpreter of the Holy Spirit.

Remember how the Lord promised that Elijah would return on earth after his death? And people asked where Elijah was. And the Lord said:

"Elijah has returned—only you do not recognize him."

The spirit of Elijah had returned in the body and soul of John the Baptist, to carry on the work of Elijah that had not been completed.

Now then, John the Baptist arrived on this planet earth, on a high human and spiritual plateau, and carried on Elijah's work—for our benefit.

And I believe the Lord means us all to evolve in the same way, with the Holy Spirit in us—and this Holy Spirit is the bond that unites us all regardless of our race, color, or creed.

This is why I am so interested in prenatal research, to ensure that a spirit can live in a healthy body and mind.

I believe that when God wants you to know something He brings it to you. He does not want you to go out and conjure up the dead to get messages from them, although I know this is possible. I believe in angels and that we are surrounded by holy im-

mortals, and I believe angels talk to me—because I have had that
experience.

I believe everything is in God's timing, not our timing, because
God alone is great enough to make good out of what appears to
us to be tragedy.

I believe God has a plan for each of us, but most of all I believe
this: If we accept the human plateau that is ours alone on this
planet earth and do His bidding and stay in harmony with our
human and spiritual plateau, then we will be in harmony with the
heartbeat of the universe.

Naturally I try to lead my life in accordance with my beliefs
and through prayer and meditation to be prepared for messages
from God and glimpses of the future.

In this book you will find the answers to many questions people
ask me about my life and thoughts.

Historians talk of antihistory when an event is seen through the
limited eyes of one writer—inevitably biased because no one person is aware of all the facts in a given situation—but in this book
you will be able to learn not only how I saw and remember the
dramatic events in my life, but how others recall them. It is a
revealing book and uncovers information that until now was hidden from the public.

Contents

Contents 15

INTRODUCTION

The Court of Enquiry

"Everything is possible . . . but the weight of evidence must be in proportion to the strangeness of the fact."

THEODORE FLOURNOY

"The people who recorded, checked, and verified Jeane Dixon's predictions are so well-known, intelligent, and scientifically-minded that their testimony cannot be dismissed. The scientific researcher will find evidence he seeks about the reach of the mind."

ARTHUR FORD
as quoted in A Gift of Prophecy

"The psychical research worker has to suspect fraud as dispassionately and with as little respect for persons, as a detective has to suspect homicidal impulses in everyone who could, on the face of it, have committed a given murder."

KENNETH RICHMOND
in Evidence of Identity

"I don't think telepathy will ever replace the telephone."

JEANE DIXON

Is God in direct contact with Jeane Dixon? And does He reveal the future to her?

If she and her admirers are to be believed, Mrs. Dixon has:

●Predicted the assassinations of President Kennedy and his brother Robert, the kidnapping of Frank Sinatra, Jr., the attempted assassination of Governor George Wallace, and the flaming deaths of three astronauts.

●Foretold as early as 1949, that Richard Nixon was destined to be President—at a time when to political insiders it wasn't even a remote possibility.

●Restored a man to health with a few words; persuaded her husband to miss a plane which later crashed, killing several on board; saved a child's life by detecting a potentially fatal illness not even the child's doctor had spotted.

●Read minds of her friends across the table, and of men half a world away in the Kremlin.

This book is an attempt to find out if these claims stand up to an objective investigation and to discover if Jeane Dixon is a prophet, psychic healer, and mind reader without equal—or is, whether she knows it or not, a fraud.

For ninety years, members of the American Society for Psychical Research, and their British counterparts, have been testing trance mediums to try to discover if their messages are proof of life after death. Their conclusion: don't know.

Research into other extrasensory areas has brought more positive results. Although it is difficult to distinguish between telepathy and clairvoyance, controlled tests indicate that one or the other, or both exist. There is strong evidence for precognition (being able to see accurately into the future).

But Jeane Dixon, the subject of this investigation, avoids tests by parapsychologists. She says her gift to foresee the future comes from God and she has neither time nor inclination to be a guinea pig. So that no one has recorded the electrical impulses of her brain during a vision, checked her blood pressure while she meditated, monitored her dreams, or persuaded her to be shut in a Faraday cage, to screen out electromagnetic waves and make sure she isn't getting her "messages" from a hidden radio. And no one, as far as I know, has put detectives on her track.

But in books and newspapers, on the radio and TV shows, Mrs. Dixon has made predictions with the assurance and gusto of an Old Testament prophet, and even described how it feels to be given a revelation directly from God Himself.

Today, Jeane Dixon is unquestionably one of the most publicized psychics in the world.

Until now there have been two approaches to her and her work: the wide-eyed eulogies as in Ruth Montgomery's *A Gift of Prophecy*, written with Mrs. Dixon, and *My Life and Prophecies*, as told to Rene Noorbergen; and the independent accounts that range from the uncritical to the satirical or even savage.

In a mixture of satire and savagery, Marcia Seligsen, writing in the *New York Times Book Review*, October 19, 1969, describes Jeane Dixon as ". . . the world's wealthiest prophetess . . . whose book *A Gift of Prophecy* is a silly, self-serving backpat consisting of creepy anecdotes wherein Mrs. Dixon foretells doom for a lot of her friends or diagnoses people's illnesses in her crystal ball after doctors have failed . . . But basically, it's the harmless rant of a lady who may or may not be psychic and may or may not be a fruit cake. . . ."

A less jaundiced view than Miss Seligsen's came from Professor Gardner Murphy. In an article titled "Direct Contacts with Past and Future: Retrocognition and Precognition," he wrote of *A Gift of Prophecy*, in the Society's Journal: "Here we have for the first time in my memory a large number of dramatic cases spelled out in quite considerable detail and with lots of names and dates. Although we don't have the type of authentication that we would like to have in psychical research, there are many cases which can be cross checked and which do indicate, apparently, a rather extraordinary capacity on the part of Mrs. Dixon to 'cut through time.'

"A number of the experiences described are of course inferable from various facts known at the time, but to pick a specific date like February 20, 1947, as the date of the separation of India and Pakistan long months before any specific evidence existed to make possible the statement of the date surely warrants our regarding the book as something more than the usual flotsam and jetsam of journalistic excitement. I would say it is too bad, as it always is, that we don't have adequate authentication—we try to do better in our own professional publications. But this does not mean we can afford to toss aside cases of more or less fully described phenomena of this type."

The history of psychic research is packed with so many accounts of the open-minded being made to look stupid by the unscrupulous, that a skeptic is entitled to ask: "Do you seriously expect me to believe that God has selected a real estate broker in Washington, D.C., and wings His way to her home to present a color TV spectacular of THE FUTURE? Would anyone but an idiot or the absolutely credulous believe that? Do YOU believe it?"

I believe Mrs. Dixon and her apparent powers are well worth investigating.

I have tried to keep an open mind.

Over the years, as a writer particularly interested in ESP, I had interviewed Mrs. Dixon many times—maybe twenty. I had had a quick, personally conducted tour of her home, where I glimpsed her twenty-five-year-old cat in the backyard, guarding what appeared to be a miniature pagoda; had admired the white marble ground floor, her canopied bed, once Empress Eugénie's, and her husband's canopied bed, once slept in by President Calvin Coolidge. Her pride in these possessions has exercised several critics. I had visited her real estate company, where her office resembles the cell of an untidy monk who corresponds with the world, and I had talked with her husband, James, a man with a strong voice and firm opinions.

I do not share Mrs. Dixon's political, philosophical, or religious beliefs. But I admire her determination. She seems to me to be pursuing what she feels to be the truth, despite the attempts of critics—some of them former friends—to discredit her.

The most fruitful and practical way to investigate Jeane Dixon, I decided, would be patterned on a court of enquiry: to get as many witnesses as possible to talk, including Mrs. Dixon herself. Their testimony would be the record and readers could judge for themselves. I first discussed the project with Jeane Dixon's secretary, Gertrude Parker, who has since died, and who was one of her most loyal and convinced supporters. She and Mrs. Dixon agreed to give me addresses and phone numbers of witnesses I wanted to question. Naturally these would tend to be people with a positive attitude to her. Others, more critical, I tracked down without help.

My approach has been sympathetic but not partisan. Although there's no such thing as a totally objective reporter, or human being for that matter, I have tried to be impartial; to let everyone have his say. I hoped, too, that I might partly answer Dr. Gardner Murphy's plea at an ASPR forum on extrasensory perception on November 20, 1965, when he said: "Where are the really adequate life history approaches? Get the life history of the person— this is the sort of thing that the clinician, the psychoanalyst, takes as a matter of course. But we have very little of this in psychical research today."

During my work on this book I found some people were disturbed because those who might have forestalled tragedies had they listened to Jeane Dixon's predictions failed to do so. Robert Kennedy, they say, could have been saved if her warnings had reached the right people and precautions had been taken. I discussed this with Edward Kennedy's press secretary, Richard Drayne. He said: "If the Kennedy family listened to all the people who sent them warnings, they'd do nothing but sit in their rooms with the curtains drawn." He agreed that Mrs. Dixon's apparent record for accurate predictions was remarkable and said that if she ever contacted him, he would see the message was passed on. Mrs. Dixon now knows this.

For those who say her successful predictions are only reported after the event and then "as told to a close friend," here are three printed before the event. In the Washington *Daily News* of October 21, 1968, Jeane Dixon predicted: "Nixon will be our next president."

In the same paper she wrote: "A wiretapping scandal which I have predicted previously is yet to come."

More recently, the Laconia *Evening Citizen* of October 22, 1975, a New Hampshire newspaper, printed extracts from a speech Mrs. Dixon gave the previous evening. Jeane Dixon is reported as telling an audience at the Colonial Theater, Laconia: "In 1983 the flag will again fly at half mast over the White House. Heads will soon roll there because of the seemingly shaky start of Ford's presidential campaign. Ford will replace a number of campaign officials early next year and will overhaul the White House staff, which will see new faces at the top level of the presidential command."

Just over a week later, on November 3, President Ford made a surprise announcement that he was firing CIA director William Colby and Secretary of Defense James Schlesinger, removing Henry Kissinger as chairman of the National Security Council, though retaining him as Secretary of State; appointing White House chief of staff Donald Rumsfeld to the post of Secretary of Defense and replacing him at the White House with Richard Cheney.

This fulfilled part of Mrs. Dixon's published prediction to the letter.

Mrs. Dixon also published in *Parade,* as early as 1956, her most famous prediction: "As for the 1960 election, Mrs. Dixon thinks it will be dominated by labor and won by a Democrat. But he will be assassinated or die in office, though not necessarily in his first term."

It was not dominated by labor.

It was won by a Democrat: John Kennedy.

He was assassinated.

But in his first term.

So there she was wrong, right, right, partly wrong. Does that cancel it out? How do we resolve the enigma?

Is Mrs. Dixon God's go-between, gifted with extrasensory perception to a dazzling degree? Or is she a shrewd, educated guesser, who makes the most of people's craving for the miraculous, of their faulty and selective memories, their gullibility and suggestibility?

Does she use her knowledge of the Washington political scene and her many well-informed friends to give her inside information about what's likely to happen?

Or is Jeane Dixon a prophet, a modern version of the biblical ancients who exhorted Jerusalem to heed their messages?

This book will attempt to find out the answer.

JEANE DIXON:
The Witnesses

1

"I Saw the Plane Was Going to Crash!"
The Independent Witness

Skeptics say that if Jeane Dixon has a "God-given gift of prophecy" what use is it? So she predicts President Kennedy and his brother Robert will be killed—and they are. In fact, a large part of her predictions is foretelling the death of the celebrated. So she's right. So what? What earthly difference does it make?

Jeane Dixon says that though the death of John Kennedy was inevitable, the deaths of Robert Kennedy, Martin Luther King, and others could have been prevented. She claims that some of her most powerful vibrations were intended to help the Kennedy family and eventually the world—but that the Kennedys rejected her warnings.

Is there, in fact, any evidence that her predictions have saved the life of anyone?

In A Gift of Prophecy she tells how, shortly after she was married, her husband was going to fly from their home in Detroit to Chicago on business. She begged him not to fly as she foresaw the plane would crash. He listened to her—and went by train. The plane did crash, killing all passengers on board.

But the only witness to this event quoted in the book, other than herself, is her husband. The date is vaguely mentioned as

just before World War II. No independent witnesses are quoted.
No cause is given for the crash.

It doesn't take a skeptic to regard this as an event with very little evidence and no documentation to authenticate it.

But did it happen? If it did, then her "gift of prophecy" does
have a purpose other than to scare.

When her husband, James Dixon, decided at the last moment
not to fly to Chicago, another man was standing in line to have
his ticket checked. He heard Dixon say he wasn't going to fly, and
he too decided to go by train.

I interviewed that man, an independent witness, as well as the
Dixons, thirty-three years after the event. Here's the evidence:

THE WITNESSES:

Jeane Dixon   James L. Dixon   George W. Hubley, Jr.

*The first witness is Jeane Dixon. I spoke with her by phone on
June 15, 1973. This is what she said:*

I had the feeling that the plane would crash days before it happened.

The minute Jimmy told me he was going to fly to Chicago, I
said: "Oh, no!" The very second. You see, that was a spontaneous
reply. I saw the plane was going to crash. I saw it as plainly as I'm
"seeing" you now, remembering how you looked from our last
meeting.

When I told him that the plane would crash, Jimmy didn't say
a single, solitary word. But when I found he had the plane tickets,
I kept after him.

[Despite her warning, James Dixon decided to fly.]

I was crying bitter tears when Jimmy left home. As far as I
knew he was going to go to the plane. He told me that he didn't
want to be late for the meeting, that it was an important business
trip to Chicago.

*Later, that same day, I questioned James L. Dixon. This is his
testimony:*

Yes, it's true; my wife was crying when I left home to catch the
plane. I got as far as the airport, but then I decided not to take

the plane. Mrs. D. had influenced me not to take the flight to Chicago. Everything happened the way she said it did.

At the time, 1940, George W. Hubley, Jr., was living in Chicago, working for the federal works agency in charge of various WPA projects. I spoke with him on June 15, 1973, and again on February 4, 1974. This was over thirty-three years after an event that he still remembered vividly, though not all details were clear to him.

He recalls:

A Mr. Keller Melton, the WPA's regional safety engineer, and I had been attending a business meeting in Detroit and were on our way back to Chicago. We got into a cab on our way to the airport. There was ice, and cars were skidding around and this was before they had deicers on planes. It also was before they had much instrument flying.

And I said to the safety engineer: "Gee, I'm not sure that I like flying in this kind of weather."

He kept pooh-poohing me. I think he said: "I'm a World War I flyer and a pretty good safety engineer and I know this isn't bad flying weather."

So I said something to the effect: "Who am I to challenge a safety man and a pilot? I don't know anything about either one. If you say so, it must be okay."

And he reassured me: "Don't worry. I wouldn't fly if it weren't perfectly safe."

We got to the airport and queued up to check in but somehow or other we got separated. There was another guy up front, between me and him, and I heard this guy say: "Give me my ticket back." And then he said to himself: "I'm not going to fly in this. I'm going to go on the train."

I overheard this and I thought: "That settles it. I don't think I'll fly either." And I said to him: "I heard what you said. I think I'll go with you. I've been worrying about this weather myself."

That man, apparently, was Mr. Dixon. But, of course, at the time I didn't know him from a load of coal. I said good-by to the safety engineer: "I'm going to chicken out on you. I'll see you in the office."

The safety engineer laughed and said: "I'll be home while you're still riding the rails."

So Mr. Dixon and I took a cab together and talked about how we were going to catch the train several hours later—something like ten or eleven o'clock. One of the arrangements they had in those days was that, because the trip took only a few hours and you got to Chicago about two or three in the morning, they switched you onto a siding and let you sleep until seven.

During our journey together I had wondered idly what had discouraged me from flying, because I'd flown hundreds of thousands of miles before that. And never once, before or since, have I ever, on my own, canceled out a flight. Flying as much as I did, I must have encountered similar weather conditions and therefore was somewhat puzzled by my own behavior.

In those days I believe you had to fly 100,000 miles on American Airlines to qualify for membership in their Admirals Club and I got a membership card, which I still carry in my billfold. That was just one airline and I flew whatever airline was available. And I've flown hundreds of thousands of miles since, but never before or since canceled a single flight.

I believe Mr. Dixon said something to me in the cab, like: "I don't like this weather."

And I said: "I don't either."

Then he said: "Besides that my wife was opposed to the flight." Or something of that sort. And I believe I kiddingly may have said something about "picking up her vibrations" warning me also not to take the flight.

Generally speaking, I am not superstitious. I really don't believe in psychic phenomena, and certainly not in premonitions and visions, but I have to admit, for some reason, when Mr. Dixon said he was stepping out of the line, that did it for me. Although when I talked about the flight to Mr. Melton before, he had convinced me that I was being overly cautious.

Mr. Dixon and I took the train to Chicago and the next morning we got off the train and I was talking to the same guy, who probably was Mr. Dixon, and we saw the paper together. And he said: "My God, look at this!"

A plane had crashed. And the headlines were about the crash.

We bought the papers and looked at them and it was the same plane we both canceled out on.

The account they read in the December 5, 1940, issue of the Chicago *Tribune was as follows:*

Six persons were killed and ten seriously injured last evening when a giant United Air Lines transport plane stalled in its glide toward a landing at Chicago airport, crashed into a house and a garage at 6350 South Keating Avenue, broke an electric power line, and then slammed its 12 tons into the ground.

Witnesses said the ship lost flying speed when about 150 feet from the ground and dropped almost vertically, bursting into flames after it struck. The fire was extinguished by firemen summoned to the scene.

Unofficial reports indicated that ice on the wings may have been responsible for the accident by causing the pilot to misjudge his landing speed.

[Safety engineer Keller Melton was listed among the injured. His death was reported later.]

Before his wife could hear the news of the crash on the radio, or read of it in newspapers, James Dixon phoned and assured her that he was safe, having taken her advice and missed the plane.

He says:

I used to listen to Mrs. D. pretty hard at all times, but particularly after this event. When I got home, I thanked her, naturally. But I thanked her as a husband to a wife. You know, husbands take a hell of a lot for granted.

George W. Hubley, Jr., says:

The family of the safety engineer told me that he survived the crash, but that he had a heart condition and he wasn't wearing any of the safety things people wear now to explain they mustn't be given certain drugs. And they gave him an Adrenalin shot after the crash. And that's what killed him.

Well, a lot of things happened to me after that. I was in the Army for the next five years during World War II. I went back to

Kentucky—I'm a Kentuckian—and got a job with the state. Then after seven or eight years I came up to Maryland to organize an economic development program.

After I'd been here awhile, Mrs. Dixon's first book, *A Gift of Prophecy*, was digested in the *Reader's Digest* (July 1965). One night I was having trouble sleeping and I asked my wife if she wouldn't read to me and she said: "What have I got to read?"

I said: "I don't know; read this book digest in *Reader's Digest*." And she started reading it—and it gave the account of the plane crash.

My wife and I both said: "My God, that's the same crash!"

And I said: "That must be the guy that canceled out the same day I did."

Well, the next morning I went to my office and Mrs. Ann Rockwell, my secretary, said: "You have a call from a Mr. Dixon."

I said: "This is too much!" But I returned the call and said: "Are you the Mr. Dixon that Jeane Dixon refers to in her book, which my wife was reading to me last night?"

He said: "Yes." He explained he wanted to talk to me. I was living in Annapolis and I'm in economic development work. Mr. Dixon said: "I'm in real estate and I want to talk to you about the growth pattern of the area of Annapolis, and I'd like to have lunch with you today and discuss the area because I'm planning to buy a hotel there."

So I said, "come on over," and when he got here I said: "This is amazing. You don't remember me, do you?" And he said: "No." I said: "I don't remember you either." But then I told him the story.

And Mr. Dixon said: "Well, for God's sake. I've been living with Mrs. D. for some years now, so I'm no longer astonished at things like this as I used to be."

2

"Nancy Will Either Kill Herself
or Someone Will Kill Her"

Shortly before World War II, the Dixons moved from California to Detroit and then in 1942 to Washington, D.C., where Dixon worked for the War Department keeping an eye out for real estate to use as depots and warehouses. They were soon being invited to parties, where very quickly it became known that Jeane Dixon could tell you your future. And from then on she was usually surrounded.

At parties for servicemen she was said to have been more in demand than the visiting movie stars, and if she sensed tragedy for the young men, she apparently kept such news from them. They left the parties, say witnesses, buoyed by her predictions and eager to tell their friends of the young woman with bright pale blue eyes and the enthusiasm of an evangelist, who only had to touch your fingertips to see what was going to happen to you.

At parties for politicians and diplomats she was less inhibited than among the servicemen and her reputation, according to *A Gift of Prophecy*, reached the White House. There is independent evidence (Estelle Friedrichs' and Elliott Roosevelt's testimony given in later chapters) that President Franklin Roosevelt sent for Jeane Dixon and asked her to tell him how much longer he had to complete his work. According to Mrs. Dixon, she warned him: not much longer.

No one is sure what year it was, but it was probably in 1944, when Jeane Dixon arrived for a charity tea at the British Embassy and was introduced to Baroness Kitty Von Ammon, a smart, striking blonde.

Witness: Baroness Kitty Von Ammon (interviewed on October 14, 1973):

I arrived at the British Embassy in a very happy mood. I was in love and had recently become engaged to the man—an American Navy commander. I was suddenly jolted out of my elation by Mrs. Dixon saying as she held my hand: "The man in your life will never marry you."

I replied: "Mrs. Dixon, this man is very deeply in love with me and we shall marry."

And Mrs. Dixon held my hand again and said quietly, but with intense conviction: "This man will never marry you. He will be taken out of your life just as quickly as he came into it."

I just didn't believe her. In fact, when she said that he wouldn't marry me, I thought she was just a little bit off the beam.

Three weeks after Jeane's prediction, a navy plane crashed into the Potomac River. There were seven in the plane. Three were rescued alive, and three bodies were recovered from the wreck. But one man was missing—the man I had planned to marry.

While divers were searching for him and there was still hope that he might be found alive, Mrs. Dixon came to see me. She told me that she "saw" him in a coffin. She was terribly sure about this.

Several days later my fiancé was found dead by a fisherman, who brought him ashore. I was so grief-stricken I didn't know what to do, but Jeane came and she sat with me the whole day long, trying to comfort me.

Jeane and I became friends and eventually she suggested I work for a while at her real estate office. And one day there she told me: "You're going to marry a man with his front teeth apart and with red hair."

And I couldn't believe it! I said: "Oh, this man will never be for me; this man with his teeth apart and red hair. I happen to like handsome men."

This time I couldn't believe her, because the man she described sounded so unattractive to me. I felt that, despite her powers, this prediction couldn't possibly come true. It seemed completely ridiculous.

But she was sure she was right. "He will be for you," Jeane said. "But he won't come into your life for two years."

Well, I forgot all about that prediction.

Two years later, in 1946, I was still working for Mrs. Dixon when an army major called the Dixon real estate office and said that he wanted to sell his home. I went to see the home and he came to the door. He introduced himself as Major George Racey Jordan. We became friendly and he invited me out several times to the Army and Navy Club and other places. As time went on I fell deeply in love with him. He was a very great and fine person; one of the nicest men I've ever known in my whole life. [He was author of a controversial best seller, *Major Jordan's Diary*.]

We were married in California on November 5, 1948.

Yes, he had red hair and he was most attractive.

Soon after we married we came back to Washington and Jeane held my wedding ring. And she said: "You will have all kinds of trouble. I just feel so terribly worried about the whole thing. There's nothing but grief."

Again she was absolutely accurate. Major Jordan had cancer and he died after years of suffering. He was in and out of hospitals for five years. He was so sick a great deal of the time. There was nothing but grief. It was very, very difficult.

But before he died there was another tragedy Jeane predicted.

My daughter, Nancy, by an earlier marriage, was separated from her husband. Nancy was a very, very, beautiful girl with all kinds of talents. Her husband wanted Nancy to go back to him, but she refused. He was an alcoholic and a potentially violent man.

I remember standing in the doorway of the real estate office with Mrs. Dixon and she told me to take Nancy with me, to get her out of town. And I tried to take her away. But children have their own lives and they will not listen to their mothers. Jeane said to me: "Nancy will either kill herself or someone will kill her."

She was so accurate.

[Not long after, Nancy's husband, Robert Dean Rogers, tried but failed to persuade Nancy to go back to him. Then he shot her fatally and killed himself.]

Jeane also predicted that my mother would die of cancer and she "saw" the figure nine in connection with her. My mother did die of cancer, at Adrian Hospital in Punxsutawney, Pennsylvania, on May 1, 1954. The room in which she died was number nine.

After that Jeane told me things would begin to get brighter for me, that after being difficult for a long time they would all wind up and it would be all right as time goes on. Well, things are getting better.

Everything Jeane has told me, and I've known her for over thirty years, has been absolutely accurate. She has never failed. This woman has been consistently right about every event in my life that she has forecast. She is one of the most fabulous human beings I've known, so spiritual and wonderful. I've never met anyone like her.

After recording the testimony of Kitty Von Ammon, I questioned Jeane Dixon.

Brian:

The way Baroness Von Ammon tells it: "I walked into the British Embassy, I was introduced to Mrs. Dixon and immediately she said: 'You're not going to marry the man with whom you're in love.'"

Jeane Dixon:

It wasn't quite like that. There were other things during the evening. I was there for the soldier boys, during the war years. And that was seven days a week at this Embassy and that Embassy. And, that's the time when I got a spy too. It's in my first book. And I *knew* he was a spy. And there was another one but I can't talk about him because—oh boy! That was something! Baroness Von Ammon wouldn't leave me alone. She'd always come back to me. But I liked her. I liked her very, very much.

And I said: "The question on your mind. No, you're not going to marry him." The question was just coming out all over her. She didn't ask it.

Why did you predict so many tragedies that she could do nothing to avert? Why did you tell her?

Jeane Dixon:

I felt that she could take such news, that it was best that she knew she had to face tragedy. And I believe there's a reason for everything. And as I said, God alone is great enough to bring good out of tragedy.

Did you know the man with red hair and the gap between his teeth before you predicted she'd marry such a man?

Jeane Dixon:

No, I never met him.

When you predicted the murder of her daughter, did you know that her daughter's husband was an alcoholic and a potentially dangerous man?

Jeane Dixon:

No. I knew nothing about their trouble.

But Kitty Von Ammon was your friend and she was worried about her daughter, Nancy, fighting with her violent and estranged husband . . . You didn't know this?

Jeane Dixon:

No, I didn't.

Why didn't you, if you were her friend? And you had mutual friends?

Jeane Dixon:

This didn't happen at the time Kitty Von Ammon was working for us. This was years later, when the daughter went with this particular boy. Baroness Von Ammon was standing in the doorway and she was going to California to marry Major Jordan and I said to her: "Take Nancy with you."

[I then asked another member of the Von Ammon family if
Mrs. Dixon could have known, by normal means, that Nancy and
her husband were fighting. Says this source, who asked to be
anonymous: "No, Mrs. Dixon could not have known at the
time."]

3

"He'll Never Put the Ring on Joan's Finger"
Supreme Court Justice Frank Murphy and His
Executive Secretary,
Eleanor (Lady Bumgardner) Wright

At fifty-six Frank Murphy, a tall, lean, beetle-browed bachelor, had been a Supreme Court Justice for nine years. Apart from a brush with labor when, as Michigan's governor, he threatened to use troops during a strike at General Motors, there was no shadow on his career; and there was no hint of scandal in his private life. He had kept his promise to his Irish-American mother never to touch alcohol, and he was rarely without the Bible she had given him when he graduated from the eighth grade.

Admired as an idealist and as the most militant fighter for civil rights on the bench, he lived up to his motto to "speak softly and hit hard." His most memorable dissent was in 1944, when he denounced as "racism" the military decision to imprison Japanese-Americans on the West Coast after the Japanese bombing of Pearl Harbor.

In his career Murphy had taken an astonishing, swift, and ever upward path. At thirty-one, in 1924, he was a judge in Detroit. Six years later he was mayor of the city, and three years after that became the last governor general and the first high commissioner of the Philippines. Four years later he was governor of Michigan, and in 1939 Murphy was appointed U. S. Attorney General. One year and two days after that he was a Supreme Court Justice.

The presidency and marriage seemed to be the only goals left for him to reach. And he was about to try one of them. He had fallen in love with Joan Cuddihy and confided their plan to marry to a few close friends and relatives.

His executive secretary, Eleanor Bumgardner (he called her Lady), was in on the secret. And when Justice Murphy left his office to go for his annual medical checkup, he gave Miss Bumgardner the wedding ring for safekeeping. She was to make sure it was there when he and his bride stood at the altar a few days later.

The marriage was set for July 24, 1949, in Michigan.

What happened next is told by Eleanor Bumgardner (now Mrs. Frank Wright). She says:

Justice Murphy had gone to the hospital for his yearly checkup in July of 1949 and a few days after that intended to marry Joan Cuddihy. He had never been married before and wanted to avoid publicity.

Jeane Dixon and I were friends and I invited her over to have lunch in the office at the Supreme Court. In fact, she was sitting in Justice Murphy's chair when I told her that he was in the hospital for a routine checkup and that he and Joan were getting married the following week.

"Oh, they'll never marry," Jeane said.

"Oh yes, they will," I answered. "I've got the ring in my purse and I'm taking it with me to Michigan."

But Jeane insisted just the same that Justice Murphy would never marry.

Later, during the lunch, she predicted that someone dear to me would pass away suddenly in a few days and that I should be prepared for the shock. She assured me that it wasn't my father or any relative.

She also told me I'd have a new position.

I told her I wouldn't work for anyone but Frank Murphy.

"You will," she said. "It's a wonderful position."

Well, of course, I should have put it all together and realized what she meant when she was so emphatic that Justice Murphy would never get married.

I said: "I like you, but you're wrong about everything."

But she was absolutely right. Within less than two weeks everything she said had come true.

Frank Murphy never left the hospital. Although he passed the checkup, he died suddenly on July 19, 1949. And we went to his funeral—on the day set for his wedding.

And as Jeane predicted, I got a new position; as roving executive secretary to all nine justices.

When I realized that everything she predicted came true, I was astonished. And I haven't doubted her since.

I was planning to go abroad in the summer of 1961 and Jeane said to me: "Don't go in the same plane as Dag Hammarskjöld." He was then secretary-general of the United Nations.

I was in Europe on September 18 that year, when I read that Hammarskjöld had died in a plane crash. Jeane told me later that it would have been useless for her to try to warn Hammarskjöld, because he would have ignored her warning.

After her first book, *A Gift of Prophecy*, came out in 1965, I sometimes traveled with her to the various places where she autographed copies of her book. I just did this as a friend to keep her company.

I remember in one place one young man stood away from the long line of people waiting to have their books autographed by Jeane. And he kept saying out loud: "I don't believe it. I don't believe she can tell me anything."

Jeane took his hand and looked at it and said: "I can tell that you've been married twice and divorced twice and it was your fault both times."

He looked at her in amazement. Then he said: "You're right."

Jeane had often predicted that I would have a late-in life marriage and every time she saw me with an escort she'd say: "He's not the right one."

When she first met me with Frank Wright, she excitedly whispered to me: "He's the right one."

Mr. Wright and I were married on December 29, 1966—and we're very happy together.

Naturally, having known Jeane before World War II and having heard her make so many extraordinary predictions that came true, I am completely convinced of her powers.

JEANE DIXON ANSWERS MY QUESTIONS

Brian:

How did you know that Justice Murphy would die a few days before his planned marriage?

Jeane Dixon:

Eleanor and I were in his office. His picture was hanging there and I sat there and Eleanor said: "He's going to be married a week from Saturday. I've got the ring." I said: "He'll never put the ring on Joan's finger"—because I was picking up his channel of destiny. And when it's destiny, that will happen. It was preordained that Justice Murphy would never marry.

And when you told Eleanor that somebody close to her was going to die, did you mean Justice Murphy?

Jeane Dixon:

Of course I did, but I didn't want to tell her. I said: "It will change your whole life." That is destiny, and in destiny, that is foreordained. We do not change that.

What made you thing Frank Wright was the right man for her?

Jeane Dixon:

I said to her: "That's the man." Through the vibrations I knew there'd be harmony there. And the other men were wrong for her and she was wrong for them. There's a harmony that is there, or isn't there. Money can't put it there if it isn't there. There's a law of harmony in the universe and we can't change that law. It's God's law.

How did you know the young man in the store had been married and divorced twice?

Jeane Dixon:

I was picking up that young man's channel of destiny. There are times when a baby's first born, I can touch that baby's fingers and tell how many times the baby's going to be married.

4

Richard Nixon's Destiny

This is the testimony of Ivy Baker Priest, who was treasurer of the United States for nine years. The interview was on October 3, 1972, when she was California state treasurer.

The first time I ever saw Jeane Dixon was during World War II. I heard her speaking to a women's group in Washington and I tremendously enjoyed her. I was so interested in her speech and afterwards I went up to meet her and tell her how much I enjoyed it. And then I chatted with her.

You know, some people it seems like you've always known them, and she and I seemed to get along and from then on we just were very good friends.

There was a mutual feeling of having known each other for a long time.

I was having lunch with Jeane in Washington, D.C., in 1949 and she said that Richard Nixon would one day be President of the United States. Now, at that time Richard Nixon had done a wonderful job as a congressman, but I'd never heard anyone even suggest that he would ever be President.

It would have been practically impossible for any political expert to pick him for the presidency. But Jeane was sure of it.

And there was no doubt in my mind that she was using her psychic talent in making that prediction.

She repeated the prediction to me in 1953, because I'd asked her about it again, and she said that she'd stick to her original prediction.

My birthday and a birthday of a good friend were on the same day so we used to combine and have one birthday party. And Jeane Dixon was there, a good friend of both of us. And someone said: "Do you have any predictions for the birthday girls?"

And Jeane said: "Well, Ivy's going to write a book."

That was the first I knew of it. I had absolutely no intention of writing a book. But I did write my autobiography about a year and a half after that and it was published in 1958.

Brian:
Is it possible that Jeane Dixon saying you were going to write a book in fact encouraged you to do it?

Mrs. Priest:
No, not at all. Because I didn't think anything about it further. Then, one day, when I was in New York, one of the editors of McGraw-Hill contacted me—I was having lunch with a friend of this editor—and I was asked to write a book.

I said: "What! Me, write a book? Look, I can't even sign my name with any degree of artistry. How d'you expect I'm going to write a book? Besides that, what would I write about?"

He said: "We think you have a very interesting career. A girl who's from a mining town in a little state out there in Utah and ultimately winds up to be treasurer of the United States. We think there's a story. And we think you should write it."

At the time I didn't even recall Jeane's little remark at the birthday that "Ivy's going to write a book."

It wasn't until we got started into the book that it came back into my mind: she said I was going to write a book and here I am writing a book.

From Mrs. Priest, I went to Mrs. Dixon to ask her why she felt twenty-one years before it happened, that Nixon would one day be President.

Jeane Dixon:

I didn't feel, I *knew* that he would be President of the United States one day and I was very sure. I had my first international news conference in 1949 and I was asked about a young man on the Hill by the name of Richard Nixon. Would he amount to anything? He was so pro-American and anti-Communist, that would he amount to anything? He was just a young congressman then, I believe, in 1949 and nobody had ever heard of the man. And I didn't get the answer immediately. I asked them to please let me meditate, and then my reply was—and Ivy Baker Priest remembers this because I told her—that one day Richard Nixon would be President of the United States, because his life was a life of destiny, and destiny cannot be denied.

Remember, I had meditated and got his channel—his channel for being. You see, we are all created for a reason, for a mission, for a purpose: in fact, his mission here was to be President of the United States.

Even after he lost the 1960 presidential race to John Kennedy, and then lost the election for governor of California, my belief in his destiny never waivered. And I told the people: "No one, but no one, is going to change it."

5

"I Told FDR He Had
Less Than Six Months to
Complete His Work"
Did President Franklin Roosevelt Consult
Jeane Dixon in the White House?

In A *Gift of Prophecy* Jeane Dixon tells how an appointment was
made for her to see President Roosevelt on a Thursday morning
in November 1944. Mrs. Dixon says that the President, then a
sick man, asked her how much time he had left and she touched
his fingertips and told him "less than six months." She also says
she predicted to him that the United States would be an ally of
Russia against China. He invited her to the White House a second time, she says, in January 1945. And then she told him he
had very little time left. He died on April 12, 1945.

Those visits have not been mentioned in books about or by
President Roosevelt or in any of the memoirs or published diaries
of people who were close to him.

I spoke with his secretary, Grace Tully, who says she made neither appointment. Another secretary, Roberta Barrows, said that
on occasion, when things were rough in the days of "Mr. Hitler,"
President Roosevelt would say "lay the cards for me." And someone would read the cards. But, she insists, it was done in a light-

hearted way to cheer him up and that he didn't take it seriously. Miss Barrows didn't know of Jeane Dixon's visits, but says "plenty of people went in the back door."

Estelle Friedrichs, administrative assistant to Franklin Roosevelt, remembers one of the days Jeane Dixon saw President Roosevelt. Mrs. Friedrichs was working in the White House at the time.

Estelle Friedrichs says:

I didn't make the appointment for Jeane but I was with her the night of the day she saw President Roosevelt. Then she just kind of closed her arms and said: "Oh, Mikey, if you only knew who I saw today, you wouldn't believe it!" Later on I had reason to believe it. Among other things she described his office accurately and I knew it so well I could walk around it in my sleep.

Brian:

There seems to have been no official record of her visits.

Friedrichs:

He would hardly want the world to be told that he was calling in a seeress. It's understandable he'd want to keep it a deep, dark secret.

Would the Secret Service have to know every visitor he had?

Friedrichs:

No, they didn't always have to be told.

I discussed this with Grace Tully, President Roosevelt's secretary, and she doesn't recall ever having made an appointment for Mrs. Dixon to visit President Roosevelt—and she couldn't understand how Jeane Dixon could have spoken with him without her knowing.

Friedrichs:

Maybe Grace Tully was at lunch or on vacation when it happened. You know, people do see the President without official appointments. I remember being in the outer office of the Oval Office of the White House with a young boy when a door opened and there was President Truman. And the young boy, to his astonishment, was introduced to President Truman, who took him into his office and gave him a pen.

Daniel St. Albin Greene, a writer for The National Observer, *has spoken to many members of the Roosevelt family, none of whom recalls hearing the President mention Jeane Dixon's visits.*

Friedrichs:

I recall having read some time that Elliott said his father had mentioned it to him. Just because Grace Tully and the Roosevelt family have no knowledge of the meeting with Jeane Dixon doesn't mean it didn't happen.

At that time my title was junior administrative assistant to the President. But I was an all-around Girl Friday.

[I pursue the question of Mrs. Dixon's visits to FDR, to Chapter 25.]

From their meeting in Washington, D.C., during World War II, Jeane Dixon and Estelle Friedrichs (nicknamed Mike) were to become good friends. And Mrs. Friedrichs can remember many times when Jeane Dixon displayed psychic ability. For instance:

Friedrichs:

One time Jeane called me up to say she's had a telegram from friends of hers who had a horse they were going to run in the Kentucky Derby. I remember sitting there at the phone and she said: "Mike, I've got to answer the telegram but I don't know how to answer it. I don't want to tell them, because I don't see that horse winning the race."

And I said: "Jeane, since you don't know much about horse racing, I'll tell you this: horses come in first, second, or third. That's win, place, or show."

And she said: "Oh, that's it! It's second. I see money around it —the horse will be second."

That was the Kentucky Derby of 1953, and the horse, Native Dancer, the favorite, and previously undefeated, came in second.

I worked for David K. Niles, on minority groups, immigration, displaced persons, and things like that, besides my regular job. I stayed on through President Truman's term of office.

About the end of January 1956, I was offered a job as secretary to Jiggs Donahue, a Washington attorney. He was Estes Kefauver's campaign manager and I asked Jeane if I should take the job. And she said: "Why, yes, sure you should. But I'll tell you right now that Kefauver will not get the nomination for the presidency. The Democratic ticket will be Stevenson-Kefauver, but they will *not* win the election."

As a matter of fact, April 26, 1956, was my husband's and my thirteenth wedding anniversary and I had the whole Kefauver crowd over to our home and Jeane read for Kefauver at that time. She told him that he wouldn't get the nomination, I'm sure. He kept on struggling and striving. But I know she spent an hour or so reading for him that night.

You know the little prayer cards Jeane has? She said: "Put this in your pocketbook." Now I've forgotten what the date was because I was carrying it in my purse and somebody stole my pocketbook, but in it she wrote: "I don't know what it means, but all I can see is MIRV." And years after that was when the multiple independently targeted re-entry vehicle came out. I had a record of this MIRV several years before it came out. And I'd kept it in my purse all that time and when I was telling people about Jeane, I'd say: "You wait. Some day you'll see what MIRV means." Well, half the people don't think anybody can see that far, or know those things. At that time Jeane didn't know the meaning either.

But she has it. She has it on the ball. And I don't know how she contains herself, seems so calm. I'd go to pieces.

When I returned to Washington in the spring of 1964, I called Jeane from downtown. I said: "Jeane, can I have lunch with you?" She said: "If you want to have lunch with me, meet me at the airport. I'm flying to Boston for a radio appearance."

So I went up to Boston and sat in the booth with her in the radio station and the public phoned in and asked questions. Later, when we left there and were being driven around the part of Boston where a site had been selected for the President Kennedy Library, she said: "Oh dear, something terrible is going to happen to the Kennedys again. It'll either be Bobby or Teddy."

Well, at that time, I guess, Bobby wasn't too popular and I

said: "I hope it won't be Teddy." She took a firm hold of my hand, looked me squarely in the eyes and said emphatically: "*It will be Teddy.*"

It wasn't a month or so after that the airplane accident happened. [Edward Kennedy's back was broken when his plane crashed on June 19, 1964.]

If Jeane Dixon said anything to you about the future, would you absolutely believe it?

Friedrichs:
I certainly would.

You wouldn't ever go against it?

Friedrichs:
No, because . . . I mean, who's 100 per cent? But Jeane, to me, has this power. And I've seen her go through many a struggle. I've been with her when I've felt sorry for her, more so than the people she was trying to help. But I thoroughly believe in her capacity.

6

"A Silver Ball Will Circle the Earth"
Martha Rountree: Television Reporter

The cliché is that reporters are hard-boiled skeptics from Missouri. The fact is that reporters come in all psychological shapes and sizes. And if three reporters see an accident, they—like other human beings—report it differently. Human equipment is prone to distort.

Many reporters, in fact, have been hoaxed, fallen for manufactured miracles and printed as fact what turned out to be fiction. When you come to think of it, a reporter is more likely to want a mystery to be genuine, a miracle to be plausible—because that makes a better story.

And even if after further investigation, the event does turn out to be the product of a con artist, or a deluded psychic, or a teen-ager out for a laugh, the reporter still triumphs, because he can demonstrate to his readers and his editor that through his perception and persistence the truth eventually prevailed.

This is only to emphasize that because a reporter attests that an event is fact that does not make it a fact.

On the other hand, whom can you trust?

Martha Rountree, a self-proclaimed "blunt-speaking down-to-earth television reporter," the granddaughter of a Baptist preacher

and mother of two teen-age daughters, is about as good a witness
as one can get—short of J. B. Rhine or the committee members of
the American Society for Psychical Research.

At nine Martha Rountree wrote her first story and entitled it
"This Crazy World." Her encounters with Jeane Dixon confirmed
her early views.

Martha (Mrs. Oliver Presbrey) Rountree made her name as
founder, producer and moderator of such TV programs as "Meet
the Press," "Washington Exclusive" and "Press Conference," in
which she explored with scientists and senators subjects of worldwide consequence.

I spoke to Mrs. Rountree several times between November 1972
and April 1974.

Martha Rountree:

Jeane Dixon has an unusual knack for being able, when she's
close enough to a person, to sense things. I think I'm psychic. I
think all women are, you know. My trouble is, when I look back I
know exactly what I should have done. But she always knows
ahead of time.

Brian:

*Do you remember the first Jeane Dixon prediction that im-
pressed you?*

Rountree:

She told me she thought Oliver, my husband, was the right guy
for me, and that I should marry him. I was engaged to somebody
else with millions. But we've had a happy life. I wouldn't change
it for a million dollars. He's been wonderful to me. Our marriage
has been happy and we have two wonderful daughters.

*Did she ever make any of her famous predictions to you, per-
sonally?*

Rountree:

I had the first Washington party that was televised by NBC.
[May 14, 1953.] Jeane Dixon was there and Joseph Davies, former Ambassador to Russia. We were sitting around a table and
we were talking about the military with a couple of military peo-

ple and that was when Jeane prophesied the first Sputnik. She said that "a silver ball going into outer space, will circle the earth and come back to Russia, landing like a dove of peace on the bald head of the short fat man." Jeane explained that after Russia launched the first orbiting object, Russia would have enormous power.

Ambassador Davies asked Jeane: "How long will Malenkov be premier of Russia?"

Jeane said: "He will be replaced by another man in slightly less than two years, a man with an oval-shaped head, wavy grey hair, a little goatee and greenish eyes."

Davies, the expert on Russia, was very skeptical about Malenkov being peacefully replaced by another leader. He said that Russian leaders either die or get shot. He didn't think anyone was going to step out of the picture.

When she talked to Davies she got very tense and her hands were almost like—you know, you take your fingers to make them as tense as you can? Like that.

I was skeptical. I read a horoscope. If it's good I believe it. If it's bad, I discount it.

But Jeane was right and Davies, the expert on Russia (who continued to be skeptical throughout the program), was wrong.

Jeane said Malenkov would be replaced in two years. He was replaced by Bulganin, in one year and eleven months. She predicted the silver ball going into outer space and circling the earth. In 1957 the Russians orbited the first man-made satellite, called Sputnik. And the following March the short, fat man [Khrushchev] Jeane described, took over from Bulganin.

I understand she warned you not to move into a house . . .

Rountree:

I bought a house in 1963 and Jeane warned me not to move into it. She'd begged me in late 1963 to get more insurance, and in 1964, when I was ready to move in and had already moved all my furniture, all our wedding presents, all my books—I had 10,-000 volumes, the finest library in the world: Everything was in that house, rugs, carpets, silver . . .

Jeane said to me: "You can't go. And if you insist—you'll be stopped! It's not the Lord's will."

Every time she told me something she'd get really like somebody who's going to leap . . . like a leopard was going to jump on you. "Don't do it!" She's so forceful and I'm a forceful person, too. She said: "Don't do it. If you want to go, don't take my godchild there."

The fact is, she was so rough on me that she irritated me and I just thought: "Oh, well, it's nuts."

The fact is we moved *everything* into that house and we lost *everything*. It burned to the ground.

Everything I had that was important to me was in the house, except my baby and my husband. And if it hadn't been that my husband was in the hospital, why my baby and all of us would have been living in that house and we would have been burned up.

Jeane said I should change the stove into an oil furnace. I was in the midst of doing that and I hadn't done it. The stoker furnace was overdone by the caretaker and that's what set the house on fire. It was an old house which had been converted, during the war, from oil to what they call a stoker furnace. And Jeane wanted me to have it reconverted to oil. But I was doing two or three national TV shows at the time and although I'd made arrangements to have it done, they were slow in doing it. It was a cold night, a blizzard as a matter of fact. Apparently the caretaker overdid it and set the house on fire and the three-hundred-year-old house went up in flames.

Was the caretaker all right?

Rountree:

He was quite safe. He was living in the tenant house.

I remember that day I stood and saw everything had fallen in, our teacups and china, my crystal from my grandparents, wedding presents. There were only three chimneys left standing. I have the pictures of it. It's the most gruesome thing you've ever seen.

I shed tears and I got icicles on my face. And all I could remember was Jeane saying: "Don't you take my goddaughter [Martha Rountree's daughter] down there! If you want to go and be a fool, don't do it! I don't want you down in that house! I'm sure it's not right yet. You've got to do what I say!"

If we hadn't listened to Jeane's warnings and had moved into the house, my child would have been burned up. They told me the fire . . . we couldn't have stopped it. It went up like paper.

None of us could have escaped. It started in the basement of the house, three hundred years old, a beautiful home. We couldn't have gotten out of it . . .

I make silly notes. I don't keep a diary but I make notes because I've talked to famous people throughout my life and I write notes down and I've kept them because, when I look back, they're very important. Jeane always told me no matter what I tried to do I couldn't retire and go to the country; that I belonged to the public. And it's so true.

Everything I did . . . I took a contract to do a syndicated series in New York and I was going to make $5,000 a week. I finally signed the contracts and I hired all the people and the syndication was broke and I was stuck with it.

I come back to Washington, I go down to the country, I take a $20,000 advance from a publisher to write a book and I'm going to write my book. I'm asked to make this speech in San Antonio, Texas, before 3,400 delegates from women's clubs and all of a sudden I tear up my speech . . . I realize I've got to do something after reading the newspapers. I change my speech and I get up and say: "We need forty million women to save the world." They vote unanimously to do it. And that's what I'm doing.

And Jeane Dixon had told me all along: "Everything you try to do for Martha will go bad. You belong to the public."

That's why my house burned down, that's why the syndicate went broke. I had to send the money back to the publisher. I got committed on this. [Leadership Foundation.]

I'd like to have a garden, I'd like to write a book . . . but every time I've tried to do something [for herself]—and I've been offered fabulous sums of money to do things—I break my leg, the house burns down, the syndication goes broke. Right now, I think, I'm doing what I'm supposed to do, as head of the Leadership Foundation.

Every time I've tried to do something that would bring personal gain to Martha—I've had a tragedy that stopped me from doing it.

Have you turned from skeptic to believer?

Rountree:

I do believe that Jeane has these uncanny, weird premonitions or predictions, I don't know what you'd call them. I myself was brought up as the granddaughter of a Baptist minister; I always thought being psychic was commonsense, but Jeane has come up with some weirdoes, believe me. She has her enemies . . . but you cannot be successful without making enemies, not personal enemies but people who are envious, and so they want to discount you. But I think, and we all have our faults . . . but I do know that Jeane Dixon is uncanny. She *scares* me sometimes.

I think you ought to say, in all fairness to me: I've spent twenty-seven months pulling together millions of women in this country to come together in a concerted effort to change the things that are breaking down all our traditions and ruining the moral climate of our country. I'm spending all my money and time on it and if Jeane Dixon told me to take out more insurance now, I'd say: "Fine, where do I get the money?"

But Jeane would probably be able to tell me that, too.

JEANE DIXON ABOUT MARTHA ROUNTREE
November 27, 1972

Brian:

Do you remember warning Martha Rountree not to move into her house?

Jeane Dixon:

I called her. It was a cold morning. There was ice and snow, and I took a taxi and I went to her house. And I told Martha and her secretary: I said: "Martha, please don't go. And if you do go, put more insurance on your house, but please don't go now." She said: "I'll take care of the insurance tomorrow." I said: "Tomorrow it will be too late." I said: "If you have to go—but please don't go, because I just see this great loss for you."

When I closed my eyes I could see and feel it . . . I just lived the whole thing. In other words it was just like living the whole thing. That was sort of destiny.

Is it possible for you to remember how you got Sputnik in your mind?

Jeane Dixon:

That was very, very easy. I was sitting to the right of the former Ambassador Joseph Davies and Mrs. Merriweather Post was sitting to his left and Martha Rountree was to my right. And Davies asked me: "How long will Malenkov stay in power?" And immediately I got that Malenkov was in less than two years. And I got a picture in technicolor of Bulganin. Then I said: "The short man." I got the letters *Kru* and the letters *chev* at the end. I said: "They're going to launch" . . . and I described it as a silver ball going into outer space. I said the Russians were going to reach for outer space military strength, followed by MIRV, which I called "the torpedo of the sky." You see, the Russians didn't change their plans. That was their thoughts, and that's telepathy.

You were getting that information from some of the Russian leaders, by telepathy?

Jeane Dixon:

That's picking it up from the air. But remember, they had great powerful NBC receiving equipment in big trucks. Now, maybe, just maybe, they were pulling these things [thoughts] in at that particular time. Then when he broke my channel [Davies interrupted her talk] it was gone [telepathic link] and I was never able to get it back again. Heaven knows how much more I would have gotten. I scolded Davies for breaking my channel.

7

"Someone Is Going to Shoot the President"
Jeane Dixon Tries to Save President Kennedy

THE WITNESSES:
Jack Anderson   Lorene Melton   Dr. F. Regis Riesenman
Eleanor Bumgardner Wright   Jeane Dixon
Estelle Friedrichs   Grace Tully   Mrs. Harley Cope

When John F. Kennedy became thirty-fifth President of the United States, the Secret Service had the names of 50,000 "dangerous" people in their card index file, any one of whom might try to kill him. Three former Presidents had been assassinated—Lincoln, Garfield, and McKinley. Theodore Roosevelt was shot in the chest, and both President Franklin Roosevelt and President Truman just escaped from attempts on their lives. There was no doubt that President Kennedy was joining a high-risk occupation.

A month before Kennedy's fatal trip to Texas, Adlai Stevenson tested the emotional climate. He went to Dallas at the invitation of the city's United Nations Association. He was shoved, booed, and spat on by anti-United Nations demonstrators, and a woman hit him with a picket sign. Stevenson, who on his arrival had said, "I believe in the forgiveness of sin and the redemption of ignorance," now grimly wiped the spittle off his face and asked: "Are these human beings or are these animals?"

Kennedy read of the incident in next morning's papers and asked special assistant Arthur Schlesinger to phone Stevenson: "Give him my sympathy and tell him we thought he was great." As they were speaking on the phone, Stevenson told Schlesinger that the atmosphere in Dallas was frightening and he thought perhaps the President should be advised to keep away. Before Schlesinger could mention this to the President, Stevenson called back and said it would be out of character for Kennedy to cancel the visit because physical danger might be involved.

Three weeks later, on November 14, 1963, Kennedy showed his scorn for caution by driving from Idlewild to Manhattan without a motorcycle escort. He enjoyed the trip. The police and Secret Service were less enthusiastic.

Five days later, Kennedy's secretary, Mrs. Evelyn Lincoln, was discussing details of the Dallas trip with him. She mentioned her husband's feeling that he should steer clear of Texas. Said Kennedy: "If they're going to get me, they'll get me even in church." That same day, Kennedy's press secretary, Pierre Salinger, opened a letter from a Dallas woman and read: "Don't let the President come down here. I'm worried about him. I think something terrible will happen to him."

Salinger replied to the letter: ". . . it would be a sad day for this country if there were any city in the United States he could not visit without fear of violence. I am confident the people of Dallas will greet him warmly."

But someone was more than afraid Kennedy's visit to Dallas would cost him his life—and that, according to witnesses, was Jeane Dixon. She, they say, was convinced of it. For weeks she had been trying to persuade people with White House contacts to tell him not to go south. As early as 1952, when Kennedy was a thirty-five-year-old congressman from Massachusetts, Jeane Dixon, say witnesses, had foreseen both his greatest triumph and his violent death.

What is the evidence?

According to Mrs. Dixon she was about to pray before a statue

of the Virgin Mary in Washington's St. Matthew's Cathedral
when she saw a vision of a tall, blue-eyed, brown-haired man,
standing in front of the White House. She sensed that he was a
Democrat, would be elected President in 1960, and would die
violently in office.

Newspaper columnist Jack Anderson first recorded the prediction after he interviewed Jeane Dixon, in his column in *Parade*
magazine in 1956. He recalled it when he wrote in *Parade* of January 12, 1964: "Eight years ago, Mrs. Jeane Dixon peered intently
into her crystal ball and focussed on the 1960s. *Parade* had invited
her to predict the future, to foretell, among other things, the outcome of the 1960 Presidential election. Our faded notes, dug up
from the files, show she replied: 'He will be an unlucky President.'
The rest of the answer was published in our May 13, 1956, issue:
'As for the 1960 election, Mrs. Dixon thinks it will be won by a
Democrat. But he will be assassinated or die in office, though not
necessarily in his first term.'"

In 1959 Jeane Dixon told a prominent Communist politician
from an Iron Curtain country (I know who he is and have spoken
with him, but promised not to reveal his identity) that the next
President would be Kennedy and that he would be killed. This
was at a time when, according to Pierre Salinger in his book *With
Kennedy*, many people with long political experience thought it
insane to believe Kennedy would be President.

Kennedy's election in 1960 verified half of Jeane Dixon's prediction. The feeling she had that he was doomed was something
Jeane Dixon couldn't shake, and she confided her fears to those
around her.

Critics say that many psychics and astrologers predicted Kennedy's assassination. Others point out that because the presidency
is a dangerous job, her prediction was just an educated guess. But
her supporters claim that Mrs. Dixon's prophecy was much more
than a guess, and their evidence is as follows:

Washington secretary Mrs. Lorene Melton (who also gave testimony that appears in Chapter 9):

Do you remember the Kennedy baby that died? [August 8,
1963.] Well, Mrs. Dixon had predicted the death of President

Kennedy and when I heard on the radio that the little baby had died, I called Jeane that morning and told her the news I'd heard on the "Today Show" and I said: "Maybe that's the death you see in the Kennedy family. D'you think that could be it?" And she said: "No, Lorene. What I see is going to happen to the President himself and he cannot avoid it."

Psychiatrist F. Regis Riesenman:

A month before President Kennedy was shot, Mrs. Dixon said to me: "It won't be long now. He's probably going to die in his first term."

Eleanor Bumgardner Wright, formerly executive secretary to Supreme Court Justice Frank Murphy and assistant to President Kennedy's sister, Eunice Shriver (Mrs. Wright also gave testimony that appears in Chapter 3):

Not long before President Kennedy was shot, Jeane and I were driving to have dinner together in her favorite restaurant, Mrs. Kay's. She never just crawls along when she's at the wheel. But this evening she was just crawling. I said: "Jeane, why are you driving so slowly?"

And she said: "All I can see is the casket over the White House."

During dinner she didn't eat and I said: "Aren't you hungry? Why aren't you eating? It's your favorite food and your favorite restaurant?"

Jeane said again: "All I can see is the casket over the White House."

She was very upset—for Jeane. She doesn't get ruffled, you know. Knowing her for so long, I've never seen her display any temper or really lose her cool.

Next day, Sunday, I called at her real estate office. She said that President Kennedy would be killed in a few days. I offered to contact Eunice Shriver but Jeane said: "Never mind. Kay Halle is speaking to some member of the family." I was relieved, because by this time I was quite convinced of Jeane's powers and thought it important that someone be contacted and warned.

Jeane Dixon recalls talking to Kay Halle, a friend of the Kennedys:

I said to her: "Kay, could you go to the White House and intercede for me? Tell Kennedy not to take a trip to the Southwest."

Kay said: "What trip to the Southwest? He's not taking a trip."

I said: "Yes, I can feel there are plans made for a trip to the Southwest and it could be Dallas."

Kay Halle did go to the White House to speak for me and when she got there she saw they were such a happy family, she said: "I just couldn't tell them. I just prayed that you were wrong." She loved them the same as I do and Kay had known Jack Kennedy since he was a baby. She's been a very good friend of the father's and knows Rose Kennedy, too."

Estelle Friedrichs, administrative assistant in the White House during the Roosevelt and Truman administrations (also see Chapter 5):

I remember it distinctly. Nine days before the assassination, on November 13, 1963, my husband and I were leaving on his birthday to spend the winter in Florida. I remember Jeane saying to me: "Do you know Kennedy's secretary, Evelyn Lincoln?" And I said: "No, I don't." She said: "Do you know Grace Tully?" I said: "Yes, I had dinner with Grace Tully last night." And Jeane said: "Will you get to Grace Tully and tell her to tell the President not to go down South? He'll be assassinated."

I said: "You mean South America?"—because at that time they were throwing tomatoes at our people.

Jeane said: "Oh, no. North America. Down in the southern United States. Tell Grace Tully to tell President Kennedy not to go, that he'll be assassinated." Now, that was November 13, 1963.

So I passed the message on to Grace Tully. I don't know what she did with it.

Grace Tully (interviewed on November 19, 1972), who had been President Franklin Roosevelt's private secretary:

On Saturday night at the Democratic dinner in Washington, I was seated quite near the head table, where I could see President

Kennedy. I wanted to say hello and ask how his father was. I knew his father quite well in Washington. It was after he had a stroke. As I started over a Secret Service man attempted to hold me up. So I just stood back until President Kennedy saw me and called out "Grace" and put his hand out, and the Secret Service man let me go over and speak to him. I asked him about his father. Then he asked me about the desk he was using in his office. He wanted me to go over to the White House and tell him whether it was the one President Roosevelt had used. I said: "It just so happens I'm coming to the White House Monday." And he said: "Be sure and see Mrs. Lincoln." And I did. And I didn't think the desk was the one President Roosevelt had used.

It was later that I met Jeane Dixon and was chatting with her at lunch or dinner and Jeane took me aside—she seemed quite worried and was very anxious—and told me her feeling about Kennedy, and that she'd like to get word to him. But, of course, I know better than to bother Presidents. But, she said, maybe I could get word to Mrs. Lincoln and give her the message and she could carry it to the President. However, it never materialized.

President Kennedy said once: "If they're going to get you, they're going to get you." So that I don't think he would have taken any notice of her warning, even if it had reached him.

Mrs. Harley Cope (interviewed on March 12, 1973), an admiral's widow, now living in La Jolla, California:

I was having lunch with Jeane Dixon and another friend at the Mayflower Hotel on November 22, 1963. As usual orchestra leader Sidney Seidenman was playing the violin, leading the trio in show tunes. Six months before Jeane had told me that President Kennedy was going to be shot and three or four days before this lunch, she told me it was coming closer and closer. Mr. Seidenman came over to our table and he leaned over and said to me very softly that the President had been shot. I looked over at Jeane and—thinking back to six months before when Jeane had literally said: "Someone is going to shoot the President"—I said: "That's what you said." She had said "kill" many times but that day she actually used the word "shoot." Sidney said: "No, I don't think he's dead, from what I've heard. I'll go and check." Then he came back and said: "No, they've taken him to the hospital and they're optimistic. He's receiving a blood transfusion."

And Jeane just sat there. She was just as white as a sheet. She said: "No, he's dead."

President Kennedy was shot at 12:30 P.M. Central standard time and pronounced dead at 1 P.M. (2 P.M. in Washington, D.C.). The first shot in the back of his neck had not been fatal. Tragically, the force of that bullet did not pitch him forward onto the floor of the car and safety. A metal back brace he wore because of a wartime injury held him upright in his seat. The next shot, in the brain, killed him.

That day Estelle Friedrichs had been to a beauty parlor and on her way home heard something about the President being shot. Her husband was waiting for her when she arrived. He had heard the news. He looked up at her, shook his head and said: "Jeane's right again."

8

"I Felt He Was in Contact with God"
Iron Curtain Diplomat and the
Reader's Digest *Executive*

"Jeane's right again," was echoed in the government office of an Iron Curtain country by one of its top officials. Seconds after that Communist politician heard that President Kennedy had been shot he recalled Jeane Dixon had predicted such an event to him —and that he had scoffed at it.

If this man were to be identified it might jeopardize his career, but I know that such a man exists; and that he confirmed the accuracy of Jeane Dixon's prophecy is verified by Harry Morgan. As a former roving editor for *Reader's Digest,* and now director of the American Council for Nationalities Service, a Manhattan-headquartered organization that helps refugees and immigrants to the U.S. become citizens, Morgan has done a lot of traveling.

In 1970 and 1971 Harry Morgan was traveling in the Soviet Union and several other Communist countries. There he met a high-ranking diplomat.

Morgan (interviewed on October 3, 1972) says:

Apparently Jeane Dixon had been a friend of this Communist diplomat's wife, when they were living in Washington. The wife had been impressed with Jeane and had been after him for months: "You've got to meet Jeane Dixon. Can't you have lunch or dinner with her?"

And this diplomat said to me: "Mr. Morgan, can you imagine me being seen anywhere, any time in Washington, D.C., with that woman? They'd say our entire government was being run by Jeane Dixon!"

The diplomat admitted that he was a skeptic and he kept putting off any meeting with Mrs. Dixon. But his wife had been very persuasive and he finally had agreed to have Jeane come over to the Embassy for lunch. He didn't say whether she had to come in the back entrance or not. But they did have lunch, the three of them. To be polite, he began asking her questions about politics and Jeane responded. This was in late 1959. Jeane predicted that Richard Nixon would be in the next year's presidential campaign.

The diplomat said to Jeane: "That's not much of a prediction. We all know that. What about the Democratic side?"

Jeane said: "A young senator from Massachusetts. His name's John Kennedy."

"I choked on my coffee," the diplomat told me, "more out of laughter than anything else, when she said Kennedy."

He replied to Jeane: "That's ridiculous. Kennedy isn't even a second-rater. He's a third-rater, if that."

Jeane not only predicted to this man that Kennedy would run, but added: "There's an enormous tragedy built into this. The young senator will not live out his term." The Communist diplomat was back in his own country when President Kennedy was assassinated and he told me: "Thirty seconds after hearing that President Kennedy had been shot, I remembered Jeane Dixon's prediction. These are the sort of things that you can remember. This is something I did not want to remember, something I did not want to believe, but, Mr. Morgan, I was there, I have all my senses, I am not senile, I am not given to all of these fairy tales and stuff. But I was there. I heard it. I don't believe it. But it *happened*."

[Harry Morgan's life was changed through meeting Jeane Dixon; whether her power with him was extrasensory or friendly guidance, he finds hard to say. Morgan was working for *Reader's Digest* when an excerpt from the first book about Jeane Dixon, *A*

Gift of Prophecy, was reprinted in the *Digest*. He was sent to Washington to see how he could help Mrs. Dixon cope with the tens of thousands of letters she received as a result of the *Digest*'s excerpt.]

Morgan continues:

I was not at all that into religion, but I respected what I thought was integrity and real honesty in terms of her faith. I remember a number of people in the office that afternoon had said: "Mrs. Dixon, I have a problem. Will you light a candle for me?" And she collected a dime here and a dime there and I found this rather amusing. But there was no playfulness on her part. She took it seriously. We went to St. Matthew's and started lighting candles and I had the most incredible sensation which I can't find words for. I can't explain it. Something happened around her. There was nothing eerie about it; it was inspirational. I was enormously impressed with the fifteen minutes we were in St. Matthew's.

We became good friends and in 1968 I was with her when she talked about the fact that I should investigate various religious thoughts and ideas, just in reading.

I didn't give it much thought, but occasionally I'd pick up a book on Buddhism or Taoism, out of curiosity. Gradually I got more and more interested.

One evening, early in 1969, I was reading into the night and it was an incredible kind of experience, for which again, I can't find words. But I began to SEE in a very personal sense, a lot of the things Jeane had been talking about for years.

After this all-night session in February—Jeane says it was February 19—I called her at about five in the morning and she was already awake, down in her kitchen making vegetable juice.

I told her I'd had the most incredible revelation, and an understanding of what the past few years of reading and thinking had to do with my life. She was delighted. For me it was an extraordinary kind of human revelation in terms of what God was in my life. It's always hard to find words for personal situations like this, but she knew what I was getting at.

She had predicted that an important change in my life would

involve going to Iron Curtain countries and indeed I did go to the Soviet Union for a month or more and to Czechoslovakia. Eventually it led to my taking American students on a goodwill tour of Czechoslovakia and Romania in 1970 and 1971. I called them "ambassadors for friendship." The first group of 120 students from three New Jersey schools spent three weeks singing in Czechoslovakia. Later I took 1,007 students to Romania. They spent three weeks traveling and singing to the Romanian people at the invitation of their government.

Years before, Jeane had predicted that I would be involved substantially in a very significant way in Eastern Europe, and that I would be walking and talking with some of the most important people in the Communist bloc. This, in fact, did happen.

Brian:

How would you answer people who say it was Mrs. Dixon's encouragement and advice that made this come about, rather than anything supernatural?

That's quite possible and I would tell them that. I think it's very easy in these days of occult interest and the TV talk shows and all the books that are written, to look at Jeane, because of her exposure as "The Washington Seeress"—to look at her only as a psychic. There's no doubt in my mind that the woman has an exceptional gift, one that I don't understand entirely. I leave that to people who can devote more of their time and energy to investigate psychic phenomena. I try to look on Jeane as a friend. The fact that she *has* this incredible gift . . . I'll let the record speak for itself.

Jeane Dixon:

Did Harry Morgan tell you about the fantastic thing in his life —that finally he was born again? At five-thirty in the morning, he called and told me. I felt that he was in contact with God then, that it was the first time he'd made it. He made it then! and, oh, the joy I feel when people experience the light of God within themselves! That's what I'm here for, that is my true commission in life. That is the joy of living, because I've experienced that. Life is different then. Life has a different meaning and with completely different values.

9

"Something's Going to Happen . . ."
Kidnapping of Frank Sinatra, Jr.

Testimony of Lorene Melton, April 18, 1974:
One time I was walking up the street with Jeane. She is small and I'm five seven and a half. And Jeane carries a very heavy pocketbook, like most of us. When I'm walking home with her, I pick up her pocketbook and carry it for her. I say: "Jeane, you're too little to carry this heavy purse."

Well, we were walking together and I yawned. Then I apologized and said: "I did a stupid thing last night. I stayed up in the wee hours and watched the 'Late Show' with Frank Sinatra."

Just when I said "Frank Sinatra," Jeane stopped; stopped on the street. I said: "What's the matter?"

Jeane said: "I don't know, but when you said 'Sinatra' I picked up something here. Something's going to happen."

I didn't know what to say. I said: "Is he going to die?"

She said: "No, not Frank. He's not going to die, not Frank himself. It's someone very close to Frank, and they're going to think he's dead. But he isn't."

About two days later the papers came out with Frank Sinatra, Jr., being kidnapped. [Kidnapped on December 9, 1963, he was returned unharmed on December 12, 1963.]

10

"You Take Those Singing Lessons"
Boston Talk Show Host Bob Kennedy

Bob Kennedy (November 16, 1972):

I'd never interviewed Jeane Dixon before and this was when she was relatively new (1965) and coming into a great deal of renown because of the Kennedy tragedy.

So she arrived at the studio of WBZ in Boston and before we went on the air we were sitting at a table . . .

At this stage in my career—I'd always been in the interviewing business—I was thinking of taking singing lessons. Just for no other reason but I thought it might be good to have it in your over-all bag of tricks. Not that I envisioned myself as a singer, but I felt, some year, somewhere along the line you may be doing a Christmas show and somebody says: "Gee, how about doing something?" And at least you're then prepared to say: "Yeh, I'll do something in the key of K," you know? I really didn't tell anybody about it. Even though I'm . . . I'm hesitating now . . . I'm loath to think that way.

Anyhow, my wife and I had talked about the singing and that was it. I talked to no one else about it.

Then Jeane Dixon came for the radio interview and sat across the table from me.

And she said: "I see something over your left shoulder. And you're hesitating about it."

I just sat there and didn't say anything.

She said: "You want to take some singing lessons. You take those singing lessons."

Now, if she had said "voice lessons," I'd have thought: "Well, after all, it might have been a good guess, thinking somebody in my business might."

But it really knocked me over. Because the way she very definitely said: "Take those singing lessons."

At that time I had a radio show and she mentioned that I would be moving over to TV within a certain period of time, which also came true.

I took the singing lessons, by the way. I called the gal the next day, who was a singing teacher, and I signed up that morning.

I interviewed Jeane Dixon again when I started a television interview show and then she said: "Remember, it was on your show I talked about the fact that the Beatles would each go their very creative ways; that these are not just noisy young men, but they're very creative."

And this, I must say, was when most adults thought of the Beatles as scrubby idiots who were destroying music.

It was a sort of high-water mark when the Boston Pops played the Beatles. Suddenly everybody turned around and said: "Wait a minute; this music is really good. Those boys, musically, are quite creative."

But before that, Mrs. Dixon was predicting that they'd break up.

Again, that isn't startling. But the fact she said they would each have their creative careers, in their own way . . . . separately.

They've all been creative. John and Yoko. John writing his books, his poetry. They've written songs. Paul McCartney is writing songs. I don't know what Ringo does.

[Bob Kennedy went from Boston to WLS-TV in Chicago, where he did two TV shows a day.]

11

"They're Going to Die by Fire"
Three Astronauts

As wife of Fred Stout, Chief of Mission Operations of the Office of Manned Space Flight, Jean Stout was at home in the exact sciences and especially the world of electronics engineering. She kept a journal and refers to it when telling of her experiences with Jeane Dixon. Although this has been recorded in *My Life and Prophecies*, here Mrs. Stout goes into greater detail and Mrs. Dixon submits to questioning.

This is Jean Stout's testimony, given in April 1974:
I'm a champion of Jeane Dixon. It's not been without cost, but then, is anything? It isn't popular, is it, to be right?

The day I first met Jeane Dixon was August 30, 1965. Her book *A Gift of Prophecy* had been published the previous Wednesday and she hadn't quite received nationwide publicity yet. Our friendship was based on something apart from Mrs. Dixon the prophet.

Her accuracy became somewhat routine and an accepted thing by me. Besides which, I had the feeling that she was for real.

Jeane has prophesied a great many things to me, which I have on record; things as carefully tabulated as where Bobby Kennedy was going to be killed—California—and when; and that was in November, months before his death. [Robert Kennedy was fatally shot on June 5, 1968.]

She predicted Martin Luther King's death to me a week before it happened. She told me, before Lyndon Johnson's famous telecast, that he would not run for a second term.

Mrs. Dixon has said that I've the gift of total recall, but I don't: I have a very carefully kept journal.

Mrs. Dixon telephoned me from Cleveland in September 1965 to say that some puzzling technical terms had come into her mind, and they appeared to be about space flight. She had the impression that they were to do with my husband, Fred, who was Chief, Mission Operations of the Office of Manned Space Flight.

She asked me to write down what she was telling me. She told me she got the impression Fred would be working over an eighty-three-hour span on what appeared to be a unit made up of two TV sets and a slide arrangement, looking like a red-hot triangle, that moved up and down.

My husband had been in the space program a relatively short time, so I was not familiar with it, and what Mrs. Dixon told me was as much Greek to me as it was to her.

My husband was stunned when I gave him Mrs. Dixon's message later that day, because he knew I was totally illiterate in such terms as Mrs. Dixon had given me, like "window" and that sort of thing.

Actually, I was so ignorant that I thought at first he must be changing his office when she said he was "going to have a new window."

He said: "This is incredible, just plain weird. How can she know about this?"

I asked him what the "slide arrangement" and "two TV sets" Jeane had mentioned could be. He said it was an accurate description of a space capsule's re-entry pattern. And the "red-hot triangle," he said, could be the module, which has to follow the graded slide when returning to our atmosphere from space, or it will burn up from excess speed.

You can check that with experts from Kennedy or anyone in the space program.

He also said her description of two TV sets was a good description of the console used in the re-entry process, in which two TV screens are used.

And he explained that "window" is a space term used to describe the time during which a spacecraft can be launched.

Over a year later, on December 20, 1966, Jeane and I were lunching together at the Mayflower Hotel in Washington. I asked her all sorts of personal questions and got no response. We were just being rather congenial at a pre-Christmas luncheon. My husband was very, very busy and there was a pre-launch set for February 1967. So I was concerned and interested in knowing how the whole program would go and how well they would achieve what they were striking for, which, of course, was the moon shot.

And I asked her most pressingly to tell me what she could about Apollo.

She thought, then said surprisingly: "You have something in your purse shaped like a cube."

And I said: "No I haven't." I had the Apollo seal on a notebook, my eternal notebook; but she said: "No, that's not it. It's cubical. Keep digging."

So I dug. And there it was. I'd either forgotten it or my husband must have dropped it in my purse when I was en route to the luncheon with Jeane. This was a tie tack that he brought back from Cape Kennedy. They sold such things to people in the Space Flight Center, at the newsstand I suppose. And it was three little figures representing the astronauts scheduled for the next space mission, Grissom, White, and Chaffee.

I found this tie tack in my purse with some astonishment, because I had no idea it was with me.

And as Jeane took it from me I saw this very marked change come over her face. She has a very sensitive face.

She said the three astronauts were going to die.

And she began citing exact dates, within two or three days of the end of January.

I said: "Jeane, that's impossible. They're not even having a shot until toward the end of February."

Jeane said: "This won't be off the ground. But," she said, "they're going to die by fire."

She used the expression "plugs-out-test," which is spacecraft terminology.

I was appalled. It was one of those things that burns into your mind. Even with a faulty memory no one has trouble remembering his exact feelings and perceptions at a time of great personal tragedy, or on hearing anything of this kind.

And I consulted with my friends, whether or not I should convey this to my husband. Because my husband had for years been in highly secret work for the Navy, I had never discussed his work with him—it was best all around that way.

However, this time I told Fred what Mrs. Dixon had predicted. He listened, but I could see he didn't take it seriously.

When the end of January came, my husband had influenza and he was at home here in McLean, Virginia. There was a large banquet. I believe Dr. Debus was here from the Cape, chief of the entire operation, and one of the Wernher von Braun team. Everybody was up from the Cape and the headquarters personnel were all at this huge banquet.

The telephone rang and it was a man in charge during Dr. Stevenson's absence. [Major General J. D. Stevenson was Mission Operations Director.]

He said: "Fred, we've lost one."

And I heard my husband very distinctly say: "My God, if we've lost one, we've lost them all! What d'you mean 'we've lost one'?"

This was January 27, exactly a month and seven days after Jeane's prophecy.

They had a plugs-out-test as it's called and they had all died by fire.

And our telephone acted as a switchboard between Cape Kennedy and that banquet, until people could position themselves at headquarters.

We didn't even turn on the television to find out if the news was over the wires.

It was incredible, and yet my husband was on the phone talking with his engineers down there and instructing them. He wasn't the prime person, but he certainly was in a position of great responsibility. And we knew the astronauts. It was very hard.

Jeane called me the morning after the tragedy and said that I should tell Fred she had the impression a screwdriver or wrench would be found at the trouble spot, among a maze of wires.

When I gave my husband Jeane's message, he said: "No one could possibly have failed to let something that obvious and that obviously serious, slip by."

About five days later there appeared on every front page in the country—I'm certain it was on the front page of the Washington *Post*; I remember it with a shudder—a photograph of this screwdriver or wrench, with a great wiry tangle about it.

[The report of the official enquiry into the fire came out two months later, in April. It revealed that a part of a wrench left by workmen had been found in the wreckage, between bundles of wiring.]

I don't think Jeane ever ceased to boggle my husband's mind. But after that tragedy he had no choice but to believe her. As a logician, as a statistician . . . use a slide rule, or any rule of thumb you like; no matter what exact science one figures it by, her facts and figures and her exact descriptions were too numerous and too correct not to be adequate indications that the woman knew what she was talking about.

I know Mrs. Dixon as well, I think, as almost anyone alive. I'm not a gullible person, but if she called me up tomorrow and said, "Don't take that trip," for example, I would unquestionably, unswervingly, do *exactly* what she said.

I questioned Mrs. Dixon as we were driving in a car from Palm Beach International Airport to the Breakers Hotel in Palm Beach, and tape-recorded our conversation.

I asked Mrs. Dixon how she got the impression that the three astronauts were going to die.

Jeane Dixon:
You ask me how I get these things. If I say: "Denis, what are two and two?" what would you say?

Brian:
   Four.

Jeane Dixon:
How did you know it?

Well, I was taught that. I learned it by rote.

Jeane Dixon:
But you just knew it, didn't you?

Yes.

Jeane Dixon:
It was right there, wasn't it? When I asked about Apollo, it was right there—the miscalculations.

When Jean Stout showed you the little tie tack with the minia-ture astronauts inside, what did you feel when you touched them?

Jeane Dixon:
First, I felt a sudden wave of pity for them, without knowing why. I realized something was going to happen. Next, I saw a fire and I said to Jean Stout: "They're going up in a puff of smoke . . ." This is a horrible, horrible thing to say . . . there is some kind of scientific law in the universe and when you're in harmony with that scientific law, you try to reach out and change it. And you can't reach out and change it. And tears start rolling down your cheeks and you think: "Why? Why can't I change it?" And you feel so unimportant, so insignificant. You think: "Why can't I help?" And that's the way I felt.

I told Jean to tell them: "If you would inspect it, not once or twice, but five times, you will find out what is wrong!" But when I "saw" the astronauts burning—that was their destiny.

When you said "it's a horrible thing to say," were you referring to seeing them go up in smoke or to the fact that you felt power-less to do anything about it?

Jeane Dixon:
Well, you see, I could have done something about it. But it was my reaction, my personal feeling at something like that happen-ing, that didn't need to happen. Although, in a way, I felt that it was their destiny—in that in fact it did happen to them. But you just try . . . inasmuch as it wasn't a revelation, you try to prevent it. Even a revelation, knowing full well it is a revelation, and being only human, you reach out in every direction just the same, to try to change it.

Now, had they inspected it as I said, not once or twice, but five times, had they done it, they would have found the cause of the fire. And it would not have happened. But they didn't do it.

When I had told Jean what was going to happen and had described the paper-thin floor the astronauts were on—that was top-secret you see. And she was telling her husband about this, as they were driving home, and he was so astonished, so shocked that I had been able to explain what was top-secret, so clearly, when I would have no way of knowing it, that he drove off the highway and parked the car.

When you first telephoned Jean Stout, it was about a month after your first having met her and that first meeting was about a week after your book A Gift of Prophecy *came out in 1965; you used expressions like "window" and "plugs-out-test." Were these expressions completely strange to you?*

Jeane Dixon:
Completely strange.

Is it at all possible you might have overheard the words on radio or TV or read them in a newspaper? Or might you have talked to scientists?

Jeane Dixon:
I'd talked to no scientists. I'd got it by extrasensory perception. And I told Jean Stout's husband: he was third in command.

And remember, everything we're saying now goes out in the air and is picked up somewhere. If there was a radio in the deepest jungle of Africa and we had a transmitter here, we could be heard in Africa; what we're saying right here in this car.

When you said "plugs-out-test" and "window," did you hear those words or see them?

Jeane Dixon:
Look at that building over there. You see it? [Yes—First National Bank of Palm Beach.] Now, close your eyes and talk about it. It's so visual, it's part of you, it stays there with you; and especially something like that. That's printed so indelibly because it's a bit of a shock.

So what when you initially "saw" the word "window" and "plugs-out-test" and that Jean Stout's husband was going to be working for "eighty-three hours" and the "flaming triangle"—you then phoned Jean Stout and told her you thought this would have some significance for her husband?

Jeane Dixon:
Yes.

When you asked to see the cube-shaped object in Jean Stout's purse, was there any chance you might have glanced in her purse and seen it there a short time before?

Jeane Dixon:
No, no. Her purse was closed.

Then you sensed that this cube-shaped object was in her purse?

Jeane Dixon:
I just asked for it. I was then a part of it, part of the thing that goes round and round and round. There are some kinds of vibrations, and when you're caught up in a thing like this, that goes round and round, you're part of it. Just as if when you're swimming in a pool of water you're part of it.

How did you know President Johnson wouldn't run for a second term?

Jeane Dixon:
That was telepathy. There were many different ways I got that. I felt that he felt very keenly that he could not negotiate peace in Vietnam, because the opposing forces had made up their minds that they would only negotiate when *they* were ready. And by picking up the minds of opposing forces; and knowing how upset President Johnson was: when he'd talk on television I'd pick up his thoughts really well. Nobody could do it, he couldn't do it, so why try? I think he felt very keenly the killing of all humanity, not just the killing of our boys.

Edgar Mitchell, pilot of the lunar module during the Apollo 14 mission, became the sixth man ever to walk on the moon, on Feb-

ruary 5, 1971. I spoke with Dr. Mitchell, who is interested in the extrasensory world, on June 20, 1975.

Mitchell:

Before space flights I have had from 100 to 150 calls from people with warnings of one sort or another. Most of them were general warnings. I did in fact check into one that was specific, but it wasn't accurate. Not one of the warnings was accurate.

This doesn't mean that I don't believe in precognition: I do. But it does mean that it is something people have not been able to control, to use at will and be specific about.

I agree that if Jeane Dixon did say there would be a fire during a plugs-out-test and that it would be on a certain date—then she was being quite specific, and it was a remarkable and, as it turned out, a tragically true example of precognition.

But even so, it wasn't specific enough. The spacecraft is huge—350 feet long—and there are millions of miles of wiring. They wouldn't have been able to examine the craft without her being much more specific—she'd have to almost pinpoint where the danger would be.

Even if another space flight were planned soon and Mrs. Dixon gave a similar prediction, they wouldn't be able to do anything about it—other than cancel the test or the flight entirely, which would never be done on the basis of a psychic warning.

But I believe that before long people might be able to harness and control their ESP—and then make specific and accurate predictions.

12

"Do as I Say or You Won't Have a Grandchild"
Jeane Dixon—Life Saver?

Some people know Jeane Dixon as a tireless, cat-and-dog-loving woman who rescues stray animals, helps support needy children, and dreams of building a children's hospital. They think of her as a friend and whirlwind, but she has never told them anything out of the ordinary about themselves, never forecast triumphs or tragedies.

Then there are others whose least move Mrs. Dixon seems able to predict. Some believe they owe their survival to her foresight. Others think she has been able to spot dangerous illnesses—that no one else has noticed—and warn them before it's too late.

Ira Walsh is one of those. He is an executive for the Hearst Corporation, a publishing empire. A few months before publication of A *Gift of Prophecy* (which was to sell in the millions and make her world famous), Ira Walsh made his first contact with her.

At that time Walsh was on loan in Washington, D.C., as special assistant to Sargent Shriver in the War Against Poverty program.

This is the testimony of Ira Walsh (interviewed several times between August 28, 1972, and April 12, 1975):

Randy Hearst told me to talk to Jeane Dixon about the possibility of her working as a columnist in the Hearst newspapers. I
met her in the Mayflower Hotel, in Washington, in January 1965,
and arranged to have breakfast with her next morning.

At the breakfast she started talking about her pet cat, that she
called MagiCat. As she was telling me about the adventures of
her cat, I thought: "It's not a bad idea for a strip."

She said: "Mr. Walsh, before you start thinking about strips in
a newspaper, let's get an artist first, with a good writer, then talk
about a strip."

I looked at her kind of funny. I thought: "Did I say something
about a strip in the newspaper or did I only think it?" Then I forgot about it and went on talking.

She was showing me some of the galleys of her new book, *A
Gift of Prophecy*, that hadn't yet been published. And I thought
to myself: "That might make a ninety-minute spectacular for television." I'm certain that I only thought it and didn't say it.

And Jeane put her hand on my hand again, and said: "Before
you start thinking about specials on television, I want you to read
the galley proofs." She definitely read my thoughts. And I blew
my stack.

I said: "Look, Mrs. Dixon, the next time you read my mind,
I'm going to pay for the breakfast and say 'thank you very much
for coming' and then I'll walk out of here; because I don't believe
in ghosts." And I started to get up and she sat me down again and
took my hand and looked at me kind of funny and said: "Ira, one
last thing I'll tell you is: why don't you see a doctor and prolong
your life?"

Now, there was no reason for me to see a doctor. I felt and
looked fit—except for being a bit overweight. And I forgot all
about it.

That was on Saturday. The following Thursday I was at lunch
with George and Randy Hearst and they both said my eyes looked
yellow. I'd noticed them start to go yellow Wednesday evening.
They asked how did I feel? I was looking for every tree and every
filling station that you can imagine and going to the john every
half-hour. And I knew that something was the matter. Randy and
George Hearst wanted me to go to the doctor and have my blood

checked—they didn't know anything about Jeane Dixon. As a matter of fact I'd forgotten all about her warning. Across the street from the Mayflower there's a medical building, and I went up on the eighth floor and saw a doctor who's an expert on blood sugar.

The doctor examined me and immediately gave me 400 ccs of insulin in both shoulders. He wanted me to go into Doctors Hospital that night, but I refused. I was running a thing called the United States Senate Youth Program for the W. R. Hearst Foundation and that Thursday night I had arranged to introduce Sargent Shriver.

So the doctor told me: "If you feel faint, I don't want you to do anything but go to Doctors Hospital. There's a room and everything else set up for you."

I was back in the doctor's office for examinations Friday morning and afternoon, Saturday morning and afternoon and on Sunday morning he gave me an examination that lasted until afternoon.

And the doctor kept shaking his head and I was as nervous as the devil. I was really scared.

On Monday he gave me the final part of the examination and then he told me the news.

He said that the sugar count in my blood was 511. I should have been in a coma when I first walked into his office, he said, because the diabetic coma zone is 280.

He told me that if I hadn't seen him or some other doctor and had my blood checked, I could have already been dead and buried.

I got back to my office in the Brown Building at about ten-thirty and I felt pretty good because the doctor said I was otherwise in good shape and that the "forced diabetes" could be cured if I went on a strict diet. I sent my secretary out for coffee. And the phone rang. I usually don't answer the phone in my office, but because my secretary was out, I picked it up and a woman said: "Is that you, Ira?"

I said: "Yes. It's me."

She said: "Thank God! Then you saw a doctor."

I said: "Who is this?"

And she said: "Jeane Dixon."

I hadn't told her anything about going to see a doctor. I was completely astonished. More scared than I ever was before.

I said to her: "Now I believe in ghosts."

The medications and diet worked. In three months I got rid of the "forced diabetes" and I haven't had it since that time.

You know, it wasn't Jeane's warning that made me go to the doctor—but there's no doubt she knew about my condition in some strange way. There was no normal way for her to know I was ill—and certainly not that my life was in danger.

For years she keeps telling me about having dreams about Teddy Roosevelt and Sargent Shriver standing together. And I told this to Sarge and he sort of said: "Oh, well."

Now, all of a sudden, here he is running for Vice-President.

I told Jeane once: "I don't believe that crystal ball of yours at all."

And she said: "Well, Ira, it makes me relax."

I know this, she can't predict something that you ask her to predict. She can only do things that she feels. For instance, did she tell you about the horse race that she predicted? I forget the name of the horse, but this horse never lost a race until this one time she predicted it was going to lose. And Jeane sent a wire to the owner and he ignored it. I saw a copy of the wire by the way. [Horse was Native Dancer. He came in second in the Kentucky Derby of 1953.]

It's unfortunate, but people force her to make predictions about themselves. For instance, my secretary, years ago, wanted to meet her. And Jeane Dixon talked with her a few minutes and then she gave me a wink. And I told my secretary: "Look, don't ask her. She can't give you the answer. She's not a phony. She just can't give you the answer and that makes her more real than anything else I know." Some people almost insist that she tell them. So many people take advantage of her that it's not even funny.

Brian:
Has she predicted anything else for you?

Yes, very funny thing. She said in January of 1972: "Ira, you're going to make a lot of money this year. You're going to be a millionaire." Well, nothing like that has happened yet, but she said it twice to me.

[I spoke with Ira Walsh again on October 6, 1973, and asked him if he were a millionaire yet. He replied: "No, things are happening, though, believe it or not. She said that before the end of the year I would hear, or become a millionaire. She sees a lot of money around me. Last time I saw her, about three months ago, she still saw money around me. Call me in about forty-five days. A couple of things are happening which I can't talk about yet." I last contacted Ira Walsh in April 1975. He was not yet a millionaire but was still hoping.]

Until you met Mrs. Dixon were you completely skeptical about ESP and mind reading and the supernatural?

I didn't believe any of them. I still really don't.

Do you believe in Jeane Dixon?

Oh, yes.

If she told you not to get on a plane?

I'd obey her. You're damn right I would!

I asked Jeane Dixon what made her advise Ira Walsh to see a doctor, although he appeared fit.

Jeane Dixon:

I felt something when I touched his hand. When a symphony is being played correctly, you hear all the sounds in harmony. But when I touched Ira Walsh's hand, I felt something in him was not in harmony with the vibrations all around him.

How did you know Walsh had been to a doctor when you phoned him?

Because, if he hadn't gone to a doctor, when I telephoned he wouldn't have been alive.

James J. Harkins is sales manager for Birchcraft Studios, a greeting card company in Rockland, Massachusetts. Twice a year, usu-

ally in the spring and fall, he goes to Washington, D.C., on business, and stays two weeks. Like several, but by no means all, who
are witnesses to Jeane Dixon's extrasensory powers, Harkins is a
Catholic, a devout man who prays and believes that prayers are
answered.

This is his testimony, given on April 6, 1974:

I met Mrs. Dixon in a Washington, D.C., restaurant at about
seven forty-five in the morning one day in September 1966. I
spoke to her in generalities and then I shook hands to say good-
by. She said: "Pray for me." I said I would. And I have.

I'd had ugly warts on my right hand for years and being a sales
manager of a greeting card company I was very conscious of them,
because my work involved meeting people and shaking hands. I
tried everything I knew of to remove the warts but nothing
helped. A couple of them were painful at times and it was em-
barrassing to me. I felt that everybody noticed them. I'd been to
doctors and they'd given me something, but it never worked.
Once, I had them burned off, but they came back.

But on this first day that I met Jeane Dixon—about two hours
after I left her—I was washing my hands and to my amazement,
my hands were perfectly clear. There wasn't a wart left. And there
wasn't a mark, except that you could see where the warts had
been because the skin was lighter.

Every one of the warts had disappeared.

[I spoke with a skin specialist, who said that warts are caused by
viruses but in some unexplained way the psychosomatic factor
sometimes comes into their cure. They can disappear in a few
hours. When pressed to give an explanation, the expert said:
"The nervous system is stimulated, that in turn stimulates the
vascular system, which causes the blood supply to diminish in the
areas and the warts just slough right off. Of course there have
been no experiments to prove this to be a fact. It's just an assump-
tion. We explain miracles logically, when in fact we don't really
know how they occur." There are also reports of warts disappear-
ing after hypnosis—but only after weeks.]

James Harkins continues:

That was my first meeting with Jeane Dixon. Eventually Jeane and I became friends and she met my wife and family and became friends with them. Every time she comes to Boston we arrange to meet her.

I had suffered with pains in my legs for about thirteen years and I'd been to at least twenty doctors about it. None could help. I had my legs X-rayed but doctors couldn't find the cause. Sometimes the pains were severe, but I learnt to live with it. When I'd go on long driving trips I'd first go to a foot specialist and he used to tape my feet and this would help. But the tape was only good for about five days. When I returned home, especially if the trip was as far as Washington, my feet and legs would be uncomfortable for probably two weeks.

On one particular trip I tried to see the foot doctor before I left, to have my feet strapped, but he wasn't available. I made the trip, but I was dreading what would happen.

I was staying at the Sheraton Park Hotel in Washington. It was June 28, 1967—a date I won't forget. I woke up at ten minutes to three and I felt a sensation that started at the top of my head, vibrations, like electrical vibrations. And it moved all the way down my body, down my legs, and out my toes. Normally I would have been frightened, but I wasn't afraid. I didn't say anything to anyone, but I felt that the pain in my legs was leaving me. I knew that if I drove home and had no pain, then something had taken place.

I drove home, stopping only for coffee and something to eat. When I got home I had no pain. And I have never had those pains since.

I'm absolutely convinced that the sudden disappearance of the warts and the pains in my legs were through the intercession of Jeane Dixon. Mrs. Dixon never told me she was a healer, but I sincerely believe she is an instrument of the Lord. There's no doubt that her prayers are very powerful.* I also believe Mrs.

---

* In the *Proceedings of the Society for Psychical Research* volume viii, Dr. Holbrook, M.D., Editor of the *Herald of Health*, of 13 and 15 Laight Street, New York, gave a firsthand account of his own sudden healing, in a letter dated July 30, 1884. Frederic Myers quoted it in his book *Human Personality and Its Survival of Bodily Death*, as follows:
    Dr. Holbrook had been quite ill with acute bronchitis which occurred every winter and spring for several years. As he was young and newly embarked on a career which was of great interest to him, he was despond-

Dixon saved my grandson's life. Some time after she'd met Jeffrey at Logan International Airport, Mrs. Dixon phoned me and said: "Mr. Harkins, I want you to have Jeffrey evaluated by the best child specialist you can get."

Jeffrey was a healthy-looking child, full of life and energy. There was never anything wrong with him. But we made an appointment with a world-renowned specialist. The doctor who recommended him was Dr. Russell F. Thompson. The specialist examined Jeffrey and detected that he had milk anemia. But he couldn't say how bad it was until he knew the results of tests.

Later that evening the specialist called my daughter, Sheila, with the news that Jeffrey had milk anemia. It hadn't reached the danger point. He drank large quantities of milk every day and it was poisoning him. Milk anemia burns up the iron in the blood, destroys the bone marrow, enlarges the heart, and can cause brain damage. It is also the cause of death in many young children, and parents never know what happened to the child.

But we got Jeffrey to the doctor just in time and if it hadn't been for Mrs. Dixon's phone call we wouldn't have taken him. Jeffrey is great now. He was five a few days ago. Mrs. Dixon loves people like nobody I've ever known. I've heard some pretty nasty swipes at her. Normally, our first reaction to somebody who hurts us is to do the same to them. She never does.

This is Mrs. Dixon's account of the event:

When I held Jeffrey McKenna I felt the same thing as with the vibrations of Ira Walsh. They were not in harmony with this universe—and if we're not in harmony, you've got to do something about it. So I said to Mr. Harkins: "Take this child to the best child specialist in the world." He said: "Why?" I said: "Do as I say or you won't have a grandchild. Sheila will lose this baby unless he sees the best doctor available."

---

ent for fear it would ultimately become chronic, and perhaps terminate his life. In this depressed condition he fell into a light sleep and seemed to see his sister, who had been dead more than twenty years. She said: Do not worry about your health, we have come to cure you; there is much yet for you to do in the world. Then she vanished, and his brain seemed to be electrified as if by a shock from a battery, not painful, but delicious. It spread downward over his entire body. He awoke and found himself well, and never again had an attack of the disease.

Mr. Harkins said: "Well, he already has a fine baby doctor and look how good Jeffrey looks and how he plays and he's plump and healthy-looking."

"Yes, he's plump, I agree. But there's something wrong. I feel a weak vibration and something has to be done." Every time I spoke to Mrs. Harkins after that, I used to say: "Did you find a doctor?"

They finally took Jeffrey to a specialist and he found out that little Jeffrey had some kind of allergy—the milk he drank was poisoning him, killing off the red corpuscles in his blood. And it was at the danger point, but not beyond it. Had it gone just a little longer, I understand, it would have been beyond the point of danger and they'd never have been able to save the child's life. So they put him on a complete change of diet and he's practically out of the woods now.

And this is my talent. And I ask nothing for it.

13

"Your Parents' Money Will Be Cut Off"
The Boomerang Fortune

Overnight, Ernest Medders proved Fitzgerald right and Hemingway wrong: the very rich *are* different from us—but only because we treat them differently. One day Medders was poor and unknown, the next he was rich and aswirl in a sea of well-wishers, champagne, and live music. Governor John Connally called on the Medderses to pay his respects. So did his attorney general, Waggoner Carr. Even the President of the United States got to know them, kissed Mrs. Medders, and gave her and Ernest a lift in his presidential plane. Medders had found that the secret of instant fame and instant friends is instant money.

He was spending millions and there was talk of billions more to come. By his reckoning he could yet make the *Guinness Book of Records*—if not as the world's richest man, as the world's quickest-richest man. And if he really wasn't any different from his poor days, then he was fooling platoons of perceptive people. Or do people respond to the smell of the moneyed, as Pavlov's dogs to the buzzer?

The Medderses' story is funny for some, tragic for others, and will doubtless provide source material for sociologists, moralists, novelists, and clergymen looking for a timeless sermon. It's also part of the Jeane Dixon story.

With a third-grade education and an uninspiring job as a mechanic's helper, Ernest Medders could truly be called unremarkable. And in a good week he took home seventy-five dollars pay.

In 1961 he was believed to be an heir to the Spindletop oil fortune, and that news gave him instant credit.

With the money he moved his family from Memphis, Tennessee, to Muenster, Texas, where he bought a ranch and began to raise black and red Angus cattle and Appaloosa horses. He threw parties with the flair of a general playing war games and determined to win. Guests were ferried to his ranch by helicopter—and the pilot wore a tuxedo. Congressmen, bankers, and Texas society trooped to Muenster to drink champagne from a fountain, hang on Ernest's few words, and dance to name bands flown in for the occasion.

His wife, Margaret, a former hospital nurse, who to some seemed the commander-in-chief of the operation, started to buy everything in sight and in the flat land of Texas that's plenty. Paris originals, furs, and jewelry arrived in bulk from Neiman-Marcus, where Margaret charged a $65,000 ring, an $80,000 necklace, and a $75,000 mink coat as if she were ordering the week's groceries. She had moved from an atmosphere of pain and poverty to a new life in which she never had to worry about money.

As a reward for joining the President's club—they gave at least $4,000—Ernest and Margaret shared a dinner and watched a movie at the White House with Lyndon Johnson. Afterwards, the President kissed Mrs. Medders on the cheek, then flew the couple back to Texas with him on *Air Force One.*

But where was the money coming from? The Spindletop fortune had not yet been released. Lawyers were reading the relevant documents as if they were the Dead Sea Scrolls. Fact was that reports of Medders being heir to a fortune that boggled even a banker's imagination lowered a few defenses. Almost $2 million of the money the Medderses were spending as if they wanted to corner the market in everything, came from—ironically—the Poor Sisters of St. Seraph of the Perpetual Adoration, Incorporated.

Happily misnamed, the Poor Sisters is a wealthy order of nuns.

Margaret Medders had worked as a nurse at St. Joseph's Hospital in Memphis, which was operated by the nursing and teaching order of the Poor Sisters. When she approached the Mother Superior with her on-the-brink-of-a-vast-inheritance story, and requested a loan to tide her over, on the understanding that it would be repaid at a very generous interest, the loans began. They reached $60,000 a month. Adding to the kitty were banks that lent the Medderses another $730,000.

They weren't splurging it all on themselves. One month they gave a charity party for crippled children; the next, a party in honor of Jeane Dixon, proceeds to her Children to Children Foundation. At that party, in November 1966, Mrs. Dixon recalls warning Margaret Medders that the money now pouring in would dry up suddenly.

If Mrs. Medders paid any attention to the warning, it wasn't apparent. The following month she hired a special train to bring her daughters and their classmates to the ranch for a Christmas party that would have made Scrooge scream.

That was the last big splurge. The Medderses had been living on borrowed money and borrowed time. As long as a year before —in 1965—the U. S. Supreme Court had thrown out the claim that the Medderses were heirs to the Spindletop oil fortune. Now they were poor once more—and $3 million in debt.

The boomerang rags-to-riches-to-rags story came to light in 1967, when Margaret Medders was brought to court by a relative who charged that Margaret and Ernest were spending a part of the inheritance to which she and about 200 others had a claim.

Then Margaret admitted there never was an inheritance and that she'd been living on other people's money. Indicted for passing a hot check for $5,600, Margaret was found guilty and given a suspended sentence.

Ernest agreed to accept bankruptcy but under a Texas law was allowed to keep his 187-acre ranch, all the furniture—including plastic banana trees—and all their clothes.

Today, the Medderses are living on investments from the sale of their $425,000 ranch, and a $261-a-month Social Security check.

But instead of twenty servants, they have to make do with a personal secretary, an office manager, a cook, a butler, two maids, and a chauffeur.

Life magazine wrote about them on April 7, 1967, in an article titled "$3,000,000 Sham . . . How Mr. and Mrs. Medders Amazed Texas," and author David Nevin said in part: "In five giddy years the Medderses ran through nearly $3 million in a spending spree that bamboozled not only the nuns but the whole state of Texas, as well. Now that the story is out, many of the rich and powerful people who knew them still find it impossible to believe. The Medderses went a step beyond Walter Mitty by turning the fantasy into sham reality—though at face value they seemed straight out of Edna Ferber's *Giant*."

Among the duped and disillusioned is Father Edward Cleary. As pastor of St. Paul's parish in Memphis he had been led to believe that the rich couple would give him $3 million to pay off the parish debt. He never saw a cent of it. Who told him they'd give him the money? He says that Jeane Dixon did. And he believes this is a case where Mrs. Dixon's psychic powers failed.

For years after their bubble burst, Ernest and Margaret Medders kept a low profile and any enterprising reporter who traced them found he had reached two people who wouldn't talk.

Then, six years after her trial, Margaret wrote a book, *The Medders Story*, subtitled, "How to borrow $3-million with no collateral and How to survive the adulation, honor, gossip, condemnation, riches and poverty." She published it herself. An insider describes it as "fairly accurate and totally uninformative."

The New York *Times* of September 16, 1973, found that Margaret was willing to talk about her book after years of self-imposed silence. They quoted her as saying: "We're just poor people who believed attorneys when they said we'd inherit $500 million and when you believe that you don't care how much you spend . . . Right now it seems hard to believe it all really happened. No, I don't miss it at all. We've been poor a lot more years than we've been rich. I just wish we had gotten the $500 million."

To find out what part Jeane Dixon had played in the Medders story, I questioned Margaret Medders; her son Frank; Father Edward Cleary; Carl Webb, an attorney and unofficial manager for the Medderses during their rich years; and Mrs. Dixon herself.

I spoke with Margaret Medders on September 19, 1973. She told me that the first she knew of Jeane Dixon was when Father Cleary sent her a copy of *A Gift of Prophecy*. Her son Frank

Medders, then ten, had a reading problem caused by dyslexia and Father Cleary suggested that Mrs. Dixon, who apparently had a gift of healing as well as prophecy, might be able to help Frank.

Like hundreds of thousands of others, Margaret Medders was impressed by the book—but when Father Cleary said he had contacted Jeane Dixon and she would be willing to see Frank, Margaret was afraid for him to go. Would Mrs. Dixon predict some tragedy for Frank or other members of the family? She stifled her fears and went with Frank. Ernest went along, too.

As Frank recalls it, Father Cleary met them at Washington airport and took them to a motel. Jeane came over next morning and said she'd like to talk to Frank alone.

Frank went to her house, where Jeane took his hand, explaining, "I'm not reading your palm, but I get vibrations from people this way."

Frank remembers her saying that his reading problem would lessen (it did), and that he would have a big argument with his brothers and sisters (he did).

Then Mrs. Dixon said to him: "Your parents' money will cut off like a water fountain."

Frank just didn't believe this one. "It would be like Fort Knox going broke," he said to her.

She insisted that it would happen, but that he was not to worry, as everything would be okay after a while.

Margaret Medders still believes in Jeane Dixon but not in the possibility of seeing the $500 million in her lifetime.

Her husband, says Margaret, hasn't given up hope.

She recalls: "After we lost all the money, Mrs. Dixon said: 'You're going to have a lot of problems but it's going to come out all right. You won't have as much money as you thought you'd get, but you will have money, and you don't need to worry.'"

It's worth noting that Jeane Dixon predicted to young Frank in November 1966 that his parents' money would be cut off. A year previously, the Texas Supreme Court, by its negative decision, had made such an event a foregone conclusion. So that Mrs. Dixon might have had normal access to that information, through a newspaper or by word of mouth.

If Margaret Medders has retained faith in anyone after her

disappointments—it's Jeane Dixon. She says: "We all love Jeane and think she's a marvelous person. She told Frank he'd invent something that would be beneficial to mankind. And that's in the future. She just did a marvelous job for him. She took more time with him because he was so little. She's very fond of children."

Father Edward Cleary, who introduced the Medderses to Jeane Dixon, is the next witness.

Father Edward Cleary (interviewed October 11, 1973 and November 25, 1973):

I'd heard of Jeane Dixon a pretty good while back. I had a problem and I said: "Well, I don't know the answer to this and I don't know anybody who can give me the answer and if Jeane Dixon can see behind things . . ." She had that reputation . . . I got in touch with her, asked her about it. We met at St. Matthew's Cathedral in Washington, D.C., one morning at Mass. We had breakfast and talked about her apparent gift of prophecy and my problem.

The end result was that Jeane didn't produce. I do know of several instances where she dealt with other people and she was right on target. Where I was concerned and the problems that I had, I'd say there was maybe about 5 per cent accuracy. These things were not about me personally, but conditions that I was into. I wanted her opinion as to whether I should continue with them, whether they made sense. I got sucked in real well.

Brian:

When you were at the Rivermont Hotel with Monsignor Shea and the Medderses, was that the time you recommended that the Medderses' son Frank should go and see Mrs. Dixon?

Father Cleary:

I recommended that his mother, Margaret Medders, should go to see Mrs. Dixon, because Margaret wanted to borrow some money. I wasn't too sure about Margaret at that time. There was all this money flowing, so there must be something here. That is when Jeane came into it. I brought the Medderses up there—I wanted Jeane Dixon to see if she could tell whether the Medderses were genuine or not, if this was a fact. Incidentally, she thought they were genuine.

Were the Medderses parishioners of yours?

Father Cleary:

No, I was connected with Margaret Medders through Carl Webb and Pat Webb. Carl was the Medderses manager in Texas. Margaret Medders promised me $3 million to pay off the parish debt, so I was very interested, for true and sure.

Now, this time we're talking about, the Medderses were expecting to come into $500 million; is that right?

Father Cleary:

They were expecting, they said, something like $4 billion; but that is what they were using as their angle to borrow money. And they did borrow over $3 million from the nuns, and much also from relatives and friends.

If they borrowed $3 million from the nuns, why would the Medderses want to ask Jeane Dixon whom else they could borrow money from?

Father Cleary:

Because Margaret knew good and well that the time was going to come when they were going to be exposed. They were looking for new avenues of money based on what they were able to get from the nuns at that time.

I understand from Frank Medders that when he went to Mrs. Dixon, she predicted that the money was going to dry up suddenly.

Father Cleary:

Baloney! If so, Frank was the only one that had that information.

She told him the money would dry up like a spring.

Father Cleary:

It was all talk. No reality. Jeane gave a talk to about 10,000 people in Harrisburg, Mississippi, saying that this would happen [the gift of $3 million]. She was talking about St. Paul's parish. There wasn't a possible chance—because the money was never in existence. Carl Webb was the one who finally broke the whole thing.

You never got the money?

Father Cleary:
Of course not. The money never existed.

Where was the money supposed to come from?

Father Cleary:
Oil well in South Texas. Some fairy tale about old Reuben Medders being connected in some way with Ernest. The government was forcing the trusts to find heirs.

Why did Jeane Dixon expect you to get $3 million from the Medderses?

Father Cleary:
Margaret told Jeane Dixon she was giving me the $3 million to pay the parish debt. Jeane Dixon believed her.

Are you amused by the whole thing, or are you shocked?

Father Cleary:
Educated is the better word. It was a great game, exciting, delightful—all the anticipation of big money. When Margaret and Ernest started showing their true colors, we got suspicious. Margaret was always protecting the source, the Sisters.

Margaret never gave one single bit of information about the hospital Sisters loaning her money in the HOPE of future gifts, because that would have been the end of the dance.

All that was known with certainty was that millions were being spent by the Medderses. They were talking in terms of a $4-billion estate. There was a little lawyer down in north Mississippi who gave them just enough legal information to make the whole thing credible. But it was a fabrication from start to finish. Margaret wouldn't let anyone ever talk to this lawyer.

Carl Webb finally got to the bottom of the mess, and found out that the whole thing was a deceit and a fraud and turned it in. That was the end of it. The key to it was this lawyer down in Mississippi. When he was found, the whole fraud was over.

You know, Margaret Medders has written a book about it.

Father Cleary:

I didn't bother to finish the first page. The same old deceit. I think that the whole thing started by a series of little coincidences. Margaret was sharp from the beginning. I do not accept the belief that she thought she was ever going to get the money. The lawyer fed her enough legalities so that she could move. She went to the nuns, made big promises, and soon started to get money. She wasn't ever going to let go after that first taste of big money.

Why d'you think the nuns were so naïve? Didn't they have advice from experts?

Father Cleary:
No. They were acting on their hunches.

God wasn't very good to them.

Father Cleary (chuckles):
God is always good. People make mistakes. The nuns blew three million.

Is there plenty more where that came from?

Father Cleary:
I don't know. For sure they are three million behind. They were going to build hospitals. I suppose there is one less hospital in this nation.

I quite seriously thought that you were going to be a witness for Jeane Dixon's miraculous powers.

Father Cleary:
I wish I could be.

But she did predict the deaths of the three astronauts. The witness to that, Jean Stout, is emphatic.

Father Cleary:
I've no doubt that things like that *did* happen. I was up in Washington, D.C., one day when Jeane Dixon was talking to a group of kids. She zeroed in on this one kid and read her like a

pro would. She picked her up. But with me [chuckles], it's a different story.

When you say "read her like a pro," what do you mean?

Father Cleary:
Someone who can tune in psychically, who can tell what's going on inside a person, who can translate vibrations into language.

So you think Jeane Dixon is psychic?

Father Cleary:
Sure. But not with the things we were dealing with—she just didn't have it for that.

And you don't think she was psychic as regards the Medderses?

Father Cleary:
Zero.

But just suppose Frank is right and that she did predict to him that the money was going to stop like a spring drying up . . .

Father Cleary:
I would say if she did say that, then she was playing the field. She would tell one person that there would be a great deal of money; she'd tell another there'd be some; she'd tell another there'd be none; she'd tell another it would be drying up. We were going out to borrow money for the Medderses at that time and Jeane thought they were good, honest people. Period. They were not.

Were they prosecuted?

Father Cleary:
She was tried and convicted, got a suspended sentence. The record is in Muenster, Texas.

You believe in psychic ability?

Father Cleary:
Yes.

In the existence of a personal devil?

Father Cleary:
There are persons who are devils.

You believe in the spirit of evil?

Father Cleary:
Spirit is necessary for the existence of both good and evil.

Then you don't believe in diabolic possession?

Father Cleary:
There are verified cases of the phenomena of what is called diabolic possession. I don't accept the usual explanations of these phenomena.

The phenomena perhaps would be insanity?

Father Cleary:
Could be. All kinds of weird things going on, levitation and whatnot.

You think levitation is possible?

Father Cleary:
Definitely.

Ever witnessed it?

Father Cleary:
I've never witnessed it, but people I would trust have, and have written of it and I see no reason to doubt that they saw it; like in the regular exorcism thing.

You surprise me. You've rather knocked me for a loop. Are you a parish priest?

Father Cleary:
I was the pastor of St. Paul's here in Memphis from 1954 until 1968. I had a heart attack at that time and am now—at sixty— officially retired. Before that I had five years in the Air Force and ten years as a parish priest in the cathedral in Nashville. I am in good standing and all's well in the world.

What do you think of Jeane Dixon and her powers or lack of powers?

Father Cleary:

Jeane is a delightful and lovely and gorgeous human being. Pleasant, outgoing, gives of her time, most enjoyable to be with. In my personal dealings with her about things where I counted her expertise and ability to see things I couldn't see, I found her to be almost a complete failure.

Have you been able to tell her that?

Father Cleary:

I don't need to tell her. She knows it. I was in Washington for four months this year. I tried to get in touch with her several times. I happened to run into her on the street. She said: "Hello and how are you? Let's get together." I got the impression she was dodging me.

Do you think she's honest?

Father Cleary:

I think she's got some deceit in her. I wouldn't say she's dishonest at all.

I suppose we all have some deceit in us.

Father Cleary:

You know, if you have a reputation, you're usually going to take the best of it, and things that would kind of pull your reputation down, why, you're going to shove them over in the corner. I'd do it. You'd do it. Everybody I know does it.

Do you think what Jeane Dixon calls her revelations from God are in fact that?

Father Cleary:

Of course not. I think they're psychic tune-in. Mind stuff. I don't see any spirituality in it. Anyone who claims they have a direct line to God is deluded.

Doesn't any Christian who prays believe he has a direct line to God?

Father Cleary:

Only in a very limited sense. God doesn't communicate to

human beings through pictures, ideas, hunches, psychic frequencies, feelings, etc.

Does God communicate to the Pope?

Father Cleary:
Of course not.

You're a fairly liberal priest, aren't you?

Father Cleary:
I'm a John Bircher.

But I thought an orthodox Roman Catholic priest believed that the Pope is God's messenger on earth.

Father Cleary:
In the teachings of the Church the Pope is the vicar of Christ on earth. This doesn't mean that he has a line to God. Our Lord might come in there and move and inspire. The infallibility matter is something else again.

But aren't there quite a few priests who believe the Pope does have a line to God?

Father Cleary:
I would say so. That would be their personal belief. The orthodox Catholic teaching is something else.

You're liberal in your religion and conservative in your politics.

Father Cleary:
I'm conservative in everything.

To spell out the problem: I'm trying to be objective; I've met Mrs. Dixon several times; I like her, but she has never impressed me personally with anything psychic, but the people I've interviewed, several witnesses to her ability, have rather astonished me. They're intelligent people, and I don't think they're lying or misled . . .

Father Cleary:
I would not make a statement about anything other than my direct experience.

Then what would be your best guess about what actually happened when Frank Medders says Jeane Dixon told him their money would dry up, that his dyslexia would go and so on? Do you think he's not remembering accurately?

Father Cleary:

I would say that if she did say that—I wouldn't say she didn't—if she did say that, she definitely said the opposite to me. She said it was *there*. She said I was going to get three million of it.

When you advised Margaret Medders to see Jeane Dixon, had Mrs. Medders already borrowed $3 million from the nuns?

Father Cleary:

She'd borrowed about a million and the money was coming in fast. She was spending it like somebody who had unlimited funds. We were all very much impressed and wanted to get in on the act.

I want to use this because I want to be objective.

Father Cleary:

I'm just shooting at you real straight because I have no quarrel. I was a big sucker. I learned a whole lot from that experience.

You're not bitter?

Father Cleary:

Not at all. I learned a huge amount. I am very grateful that I was conned and suckered, because I haven't been since.

Did you learn that most people are greedy?

Father Cleary:

Not so much. There was quite a bit of good solid Christian charity among some. Great humanitarianism among a few. But the vast majority went with the buck.

But Mrs. Medders told me—I know you don't trust her—that they kept most of their old friends, even after they lost all the money.

Father Cleary:

Ho, ho, ho, ho!

*Attorney Carl E. Webb, described as manager for the Med-
derses by Father Edward Cleary, did not want to talk about the
Medderses—but he was prepared to discuss Jeane Dixon:*

Attorney Carl E. Webb, March 28, 1974:

I was in and out of Washington on several occasions and was
there for as long as a week on one occasion and went to Mass
with Mrs. Dixon, and sat with her in her office and opened her
mail for four, five days on one occasion.

Did she predict anything to you that came true?

Webb:

Not really. I'm not a very mystical type person anyway. I would
not have been the type of person that would be seeking that type
of thing. I would be somewhat skeptical, and I guess, as I say, I'm
by nature that way. Anyway, one interesting little thing, a side-
light: Mrs. Dixon did tell me on one occasion that I was very subject to injuries of the hand. And my wife and I laugh at it frequently, because, for one thing, about twelve years ago I had very
severe injuries to my hand in an automobile accident and frequently since then it seems I am the type of person who cannot
do anything without injuring my hand.

*Was there any evidence when she saw you that your hand was
scarred or anything?*

Webb:
No, there was not.

That's remarkable, isn't it?

Webb:
Yes, it's remarkable.

Do you think then that Jeane Dixon has got something?

Webb:
Yes, I think she has a gift, to some degree.

Jeane Dixon on the Medderses:

It wasn't only the very old attorney who persuaded the
Medderses they would get the Spindletop fortune. There was an-

other, very reputable attorney representing them, as well. And on the strength of that the Medderses were able to borrow from banks.

Margaret Medders did intend to give Father Cleary the $3 million. It was in her mind to do so—until, of course, she hadn't any to give.

I still believe the Medderses will get a great deal of money, but not as much as they had hoped for; not the $500 million.

14

"Proud Clarion Will Win the Kentucky Derby" Richest Man in the World Asks Jeane Dixon to Help Him Make More

My phone rang. H. L. Hunt was on the line. His secretary had passed on my message that I was writing a book about Jeane Dixon—and he was willing to discuss his encounters with her.

He died a year after the interview.

Comparisons seem necessary to visualize how rich Hunt was. His company, for example, produced more oil in World War II than *all* enemy countries put together. And educated guessers said that had he given away to 4,000 people one million dollars each, Hunt still would have had enough left to call himself a billionaire. He lived in a replica of George Washington's Mount Vernon, except that Hunt's house was bigger. Yet in many ways he lived modestly, taking his lunch to work in a paper bag.

He shared with Aristotle Onassis—the only other billionaire I've spoken with—a quiet, unemphatic voice—that of a man who never needs to shout to get attention. I told him I'd tape our conversation to avoid any misquoting, checked to see that the equipment was working, and then mostly listened.

This is H. L. Hunt's testimony, given on March 4, 1974:

I first met Jeane Dixon in the spring of 1967, when she gave a talk to 380 army officers' wives at Fort Myer, Virginia. And I went along with her. She began speaking about horses and someone in the audience asked her which horse would win the Kentucky Derby, which was to run the next Saturday.

She answered: "It will be Proud Clarion, in the post position seven."

Now, the post positions had not even been decided on yet. There were fourteen horses in the race, so the odds against Proud Clarion even getting that post position were thirteen to one.

That Saturday I watched the Derby on television and found that Proud Clarion had been given post position seven.

And—need I add—Proud Clarion won the race, paying $62.20 for a $2 ticket. Those are odds of 30 to 1. And the 30 to 1 odds multiplied by the 13 to 1, make the odds against the completion of the entire prophecy 390 to 1.

But some of Jeane Dixon's prophecies have come true against odds much greater than those.

At one time I was considering bidding with a combine of other oil operators on an oil deal. Before I entered the deal I asked Jeane for her advice. She predicted that numerous complications and problems would develop in the project. There would be troublesome controversies and disputes, she warned.

I chose not to bid. And her predictions turned out to be true. All sorts of troubles developed in that deal, and I wasn't part of it.

Because I found, on this and other occasions, that her advice was always constructive, I called her on another important project.

About four years ago I was considering making a bid on an offshore area of 5,000 acres. There were a number of such tracts available and my geologists reported that four of them were worth consideration.

I asked Jeane for her advice; which one of them would turn out best of all?

She told me to bid for one specific tract—number 207—and to make sure that we got it.

"Don't try to buy it for a song," she said. "Bid high enough to make it positive you'll get it."

I took her advice. Our bid was substantially above that of the next highest bidder. So we got it.

And that lot 207 turned out to be the best in the entire area. It was a hugely profitable tract.

Only four years since we got it I believe it's already paid for itself.

Although I didn't bet on that Kentucky Derby winner she predicted, I've never failed to take her advice since that time.

As a seeress she's fantastic—and she's without equal. To say that her prophecies are amazingly accurate, in my opinion, would be the understatement of the year.

I think Jeane Dixon is a very remarkable woman, and a good woman.

If there was something very important in my life or work to be decided, and technical answers weren't satisfactory, I would value her advice.

I asked Jeane Dixon how she got the Derby winner and the post positions.

Jeane Dixon:

The name and number just came into my head and I knew at once that they were right. As for the lot I told him to bid on— 207—I meditated a long time before I knew that was the one. I understand it made millions of dollars for him.

How would you answer those who ask you: "Why do you use your God-given gift to help a billionaire make more millions?"

Jeane Dixon:

I help all sorts of people, but the papers only want to write about people like H. L. Hunt. If you came to my office you'd see the people that I help, the little people; finding missing children. Today, I got seven letters about missing youngsters. Yesterday I got eleven. Remember, in one day, eleven. I don't have time even to meditate on missing people. I help little people; helping them to help themselves, people who don't make the newspapers.

I help my friends, too. And H. L. Hunt is a friend of mine.

I had a question given to me one day before a big audience of

about three thousand people, and I guess they had it in for Howard Hughes. And the question was: "Don't you think the law
should change in America so one person could not build up an
empire and make as much money as Howard Hughes?"

So I thought a moment, and I said: "This is not a psychic answer. This is just a commonsense answer. I would say I would
never ask them to change the law, because if it wasn't for Howard
Hughes there would be 340,000 people out of work. Howard
Hughes cannot take it with him. And he's going to leave all he
has to prenatal research, so that the Holy Spirit can live in normal
bodies." I said: "We should have more Howard Hugheses, so we
can have more jobs and there'd be more money left for charity to
do great things with. So, if he wants to make more money, let him
make more money, because he can't take it with him."

*I think a hardheaded answer to that would be that the money
he's got now might have been spent on prenatal research twenty
years earlier—if it had been taken away from him.*

Jeane Dixon:
But you can't take all this money and give it to the poor, and
tear down all the churches. Because the poor are always with us.
Because that's the law. Because they're on this human plateau,
they have to build up and build up and earn and earn and earn.
You take all the riches of H. L. Hunt, put it together with
Hughes's, and give it to the poor—and how long would it last?

15

"Tell Rose to Keep Bobby Out of This Hotel"
Death of Robert Kennedy

THE WITNESSES:
James Fahey   Estelle Friedrichs   Frank Boykin
June Wright   Erny Pinckert   Ira Walsh   Tom Swafford

Before plane flights on the 1968 campaign trail, Robert Kennedy drove around in an open convertible and gave himself to the crowds. He was mauled by frenzied strangers and as it was impossible to distinguish fans from foes, Kennedy told his volunteer bodyguards to go easy on everyone. When hands failed to reach out for him, he reached out. The collectors grabbed for his clothes and he returned to his plane one evening, wet with perspiration, minus tie, cuff links, and one shoe, looking more like a young Bowery bum than a presidential candidate. "Don't tell me the people in this country don't love me," he said as he dropped wearily into his seat. "On the other hand, perhaps all they wanted was my shoe."

Once, Associated Press reporter Joseph Mohbat sat next to him on the plane and asked the question that was on the minds of millions. Did Robert Kennedy ever consider the possibility of assassination? Yes, he said, he did. But he wasn't going to change his campaign style because of that. He felt that he had to get close to people.

"After all," said TV newsman Roger Mudd to this writer, "it's hard to campaign as a 'candidate of the people' if you arrive surrounded by a phalanx of helmets, night clubs, and billy sticks and men in polished leather boots."

So Robert Kennedy took chances.

By turns elated and exhausted, calling politics "an honorable adventure" as if to reassure himself it was all worth it, he moved closer to his goal of the White House, and as he did his friends grew increasingly fearful for him.

"You felt he was doomed and you knew he felt it," said Robert Lowell. And Jacqueline Kennedy told Arthur Schlesinger: "If Bobby becomes President, they'd do to him what they did to Jack."

Jeane Dixon had premonitions that Robert Kennedy would be killed, visions of his dying, a feeling at one time that he would commit suicide, impressions that a group were plotting his death —but she sensed that these were man-made plans and could be changed. RFK could be saved, she believed, if only she could get to him with a warning.

Her many attempts to warn President Kennedy, according to firsthand witnesses, had failed. She had made the effort even though sensing his assassination was inevitable—his destiny. But his brother Robert was another matter. She believed he could be saved.

Mrs. Dixon turned to James Fahey for help. Fahey, born in New York's Hell's Kitchen, and an orphan at two, had served in the Navy in the South Pacific during World War II, fighting much the same war as President Kennedy. He teamed up with the President when he was on PT Boat 109 and also PT Boat 59 during the Solomon Islands campaign. Fahey was a Kennedy family buff. As a superhuman labor of love, he had gone through some 300,000 newspaper pages searching for items about the Kennedys from 1892 and the days of Honey Fitz, to the days of John and Robert. The newspaper collection was then converted into

nineteen rolls of microfilm, and Fahey gave the first set to the
Library of Congress and, later on, a set to the Kennedy Memorial
Library in Waltham, Massachusetts.

Jeane Dixon couldn't have chosen much better than James
Fahey to make contact with Robert Kennedy for her. Fahey was
an honest man with no political ambitions. His motives were pat-
ently pure. Senator Kennedy knew him to be a friend. In fact, he
had once autographed his book *Just Friends and Brave Enemies*
with the words: "For Jim Fahey who has been such a good friend
of all the Kennedys." Although an autograph is not an affidavit,
this one rang true.

The biggest hurdle, Mrs. Dixon believed, was the first, to get
Robert Kennedy to listen to her. If the news ever leaked out that
a politician with presidential aspirations was taking advice from a
psychic, it would lose him some supporters for sure and drive critics to derision. That in itself, of course, might have knocked him
out of the running and thereby saved his life; but it's a big "might."

Go-between James Fahey had written a best seller about his
World War II experiences, *Pacific War Diary*; and with the royalties he built a cathedral in South India, all the while continuing
to work as a garbage collector for his hometown, Waltham, Massachusetts. Later on, in 1970, Pope Paul VI gave Fahey and his
wife an audience and said of his generosity, "What you have done
will last for a thousand years."

President Kennedy invited Fahey to the White House on September 10, 1963, when he accepted an autographed copy of *Pacific
War Diary '42–45* and autographed a copy of his own book,
Profiles in Courage, as follows: "To James Fahey who brings it all
back." Then he handed Fahey his pen to keep.

Jim Fahey was carrying this pen when he met Jeane Dixon. He
had first heard Mrs. Dixon speak when she was interviewed on a
Boston radio program by Bob Kennedy (no relation, and also a
witness in Chapter 10), and Fahey felt intuitively that he would
meet her one day.

President Kennedy was killed less than three months after
Fahey exchanged books with him. Fahey attended the funeral and
has returned to Arlington National Cemetery each anniversary to

put flowers on the President's grave. And that is what brought Fahey to Washington from Waltham in September 1965.

This is James Fahey's testimony:

I was walking down the street when I saw a sign at Woodward and Lothrop department store saying that Jeane Dixon was autographing her book *A Gift of Prophecy*; so I went inside the store. There was a big mob of people, so large that I was discouraged and ready to turn away. But something held me there and told me, "Why don't you go around the crowd and see how she autographs the book?" So I went around and was right behind her and saw that she always wrote down "God bless you." It really moved me; so I stayed there.

When the autograph party was almost over, I gave her a copy of her book which I had just bought and asked her to autograph it. When I told her that the pen I handed her was the same pen that President Kennedy had used, she was thrilled, you know. After the crowd left, I had a chat with her; and that's how it all started. My wife and I have become very close to Jeane; and when we go back every year to Washington, we always visit her.

I saw Jeane on September 13, 1967, and she gave me an autographed copy of *A Gift of Prophecy* and asked me to give it to Bobby Kennedy. She also asked me to give him a message that she must see him about something very important.

Senator Kennedy was a very easy person to get to; he couldn't do enough for people. I just went to his office, as I had many times before, and said I wanted to see him; and a few moments later I was asked in. First, I gave him Jeane Dixon's book, and then I put it bluntly to him: "She wants to see you. It's very important."

Bobby was standing facing me in his office. There was nothing but a long period of silence as he kept staring at the floor. I couldn't read his mind, but I knew he wasn't going to answer me that day. I finally told him that I had another appointment to see his friend Senator Ralph Yarborough of Texas, and left.

Jeane was very disappointed when I went back and explained what had happened. I wrote Bobby later that same year suggesting that he meet Jeane Dixon, but he didn't reply. Six months later, on March 4, 1968, I again visited Bobby Kennedy in his Washington office. It was just before St. Patrick's Day, and I'd bought a gift for him, a plaque with an Irish toast on it. On the right side of the plaque was a statue of St. Patrick, and on the left were the words: "May you be in heaven a half-hour before the Devil knows you're dead." The lady in the store who sold it to me said, "There's a funny one." It struck me as funny, too, because the Irish have a great sense of humor and like to joke about themselves.

Bobby read it in a very serious mood and didn't say a word. I was disappointed. I expected him to laugh. His reaction of silence was the same as when I had told him that Jeane Dixon wanted to see him. He just stared at the words of the toast for a long time before he looked up, and he said nothing. On this occasion, I again asked him to see Jeane Dixon, but he would not answer.

I told him I'd like to have my photograph taken with him, and he asked if I had a camera. When I said "no," he said "not to worry," he'd arrange for that and to meet him the next day. He was coming back from a meeting when I met him next afternoon on the Capitol steps, and that's where we had our photograph taken together by an official photographer, I believe. That was on March 5, three months to the day he was shot.

I last saw Bobby on March 17, 1968, when he was in the St. Patrick's Day parade in South Boston. He spotted me in the crowd as he was passing by in a police car and yelled, "Jim! Jim!" as he waved to me; and then he was gone.

Estelle Friedrichs testifies:

In April or May of 1968, weeks before it happened, Jeane told me she had seen the exact spot where Bobby Kennedy would be shot. She said it would be in California. She said she saw blood all over the place, and there would be a mob of people around him.

On April 4, 1968, Jeane Dixon was lunching on the roof of the Washington Hotel in Washington, D.C., with Frank William Boykin, former U. S. Congressman for Alabama (he has since died), and his wife.

Frank Boykin testified:

We were lunching together and Mrs. Dixon said that Robert

Kennedy would be shot in California. She said she got a clear picture that he would be shot and wounded but she didn't know if he would recover. I know she told many mutual friends of her mental vision that Robert Kennedy would be shot and they told her it would be useless to warn him—that he wouldn't be receptive to such a warning.

But, in fact, Jeane Dixon didn't give up trying to warn RFK, nor did James Fahey.

Fahey resumes his testimony:

On May 27, 1968, nine days before the assassination, I dropped in on my good friend Dave Powers, at his office at the Federal Records Center at Waltham, Massachusetts. This is where the Kennedy Memorial Library is temporarily located. Dave was not only one of President Kennedy's White House aides, but also a good friend. He was closer to President Kennedy than anyone and was with him continuously, even in Dallas when he was shot; and Dave also co-authored the book about him *Johnny, We Hardly Knew Ye.*

Anyway, I ran to see him because he was just getting into his car in the parking lot. He told me he was leaving for Ireland in a couple of days with Joan and Eunice Kennedy for the dedication of the President Kennedy Park in Ireland. I told him: "If you knew what Jeane Dixon said about Bobby Kennedy, it would knock you over." She had told me that it was a matter of life and death.

I explained to Dave that Jeane Dixon wanted to see Bobby and suggested that Dave ask Joan Kennedy on the way to Ireland to arrange a meeting between the Kennedys and Jeane Dixon. Dave said he would try.

In Los Angeles, Sirhan Sirhan, a Palestinian Arab, bitterly angry over the outcome of the Israeli-Arab wars and apparent United States support of Israel, had bought a gun and was dabbling in the occult. He stared into a mirror, while half-consciously scrawling in a notebook his intention to kill Robert Kennedy; associating Kennedy with the pro-Israelis; writing the words over and over again:

"R.F.K. must die RFK must be killed R.F.K. must be assassi-nated." *as if repetition could spur him to the act. Sirhan believed, it is said, that he could change the colors of a candle flame by willing it to change, and once, by thinking hard, was convinced that he woke his sleeping mother and directed her with his mind to go to the bathroom.*

On May 28, 1968, Sirhan looked in on a meeting of the Akhra-ton Chapter of the Ancient Mystical Order of Rosae Crusis, in Pasadena, attracted there by his growing fascination with the oc-cult.

That same day, and the day after James Fahey had spoken with Dave Powers, Jeane Dixon landed at Los Angeles airport. Her friend June Wright, an ex-newspaperwoman, widow of public relations executive Chester Wright, and mother of an attorney, was waiting to meet her.

June Wright testifies on January 31, 1974:

Jeane was going to give a speech at a luncheon before 400 members of the Women's Auxiliary to the Medical Association of Los Angeles. I met her at the airport with Mrs. Ramona Luck, head of the auxiliary. We drove to Mrs. Luck's home on Wilshire Boulevard for Jeane to change clothes—then Mrs. Luck drove us to the Ambassador Hotel. Jeane was to speak in the Embassy Room.

We were very late when we arrived and because of that Jeane was very nervous. The Kennedys were all at the Ambassador and there was also a huge bridge tournament going on. The place was jammed with people.

Before we went into the Ambassador Hotel Jeane said to me: "Why don't you call Rose Kennedy? You know her. Get her to come down here and listen to my talk." I don't think before we went into that hotel Jeane had any indication of anything that was going to happen. I said: "Oh, you know she hates to come to these things. She doesn't want to be seen, and she doesn't like to have people talking to her at this time." And Jeane said: "Oh, tell her to put on some dark glasses and come listen to my talk."

We were so late when we arrived, I said: "You two go on in there, because we're late. I'll wait until I get a parking ticket for the car." Which I did.

When I got inside the dining room I was seated at a table with newspaper people. And Jeane immediately beckoned to me to join her up on the stage. When I got there she seemed very upset and she whispered: "I don't think I can keep my mind on my speech. All I can see is a black cloud of Bobby Kennedy's body going from here up through the ceiling." [She was seated directly in front of the door to the kitchen where Bobby was later shot.] And she waved her hand and described it as "like smoke going up," I think. I understood she meant that he would be killed. Of course I'd heard her talk so much about John Kennedy and how she'd tried so many times to warn the White House to keep him away from Dallas.

Captain George Maines, a public relations man with us, heard her and said: "Jeane, *forget it*. Keep your mind on what you've come here for!"

And I said to her: "Forget it. Just forget it and go on with your speech."

But she was very, very nervous during the whole thing. When one of the audience asked if Robert Kennedy would be President, she answered that he would never be President of the United States.

They had a new manager at the Ambassador Hotel who had just come from the Washington Hilton in Washington, D.C., and Jeane said to me after the luncheon: "I'm going to tell him."

I said: "Jeane, I wouldn't if I were you. Why upset the man and make him nervous on his new job?" George Maines also implored her not to mention it to the new manager.

So she didn't say anything to him. But she kept on repeating to me, two or three times, that all she could see was a cloud of Bobby Kennedy's body going up through the ceiling.

George Maines and I tried to calm her down and get her to forget it. But she wouldn't. She said to me: "June, why don't you try to get Rose Kennedy and tell her to keep Bobby out of this hotel? Tell her there are bad omens here."

I said I'd try.

Erny Pinckert, Jeane Dixon's brother, testifies on October 27, 1973:

I was sitting in the audience, about twenty feet away from Jeane, at the second row of tables.

Jeane was on the same rostrum and in the same position as Robert Kennedy when he appeared later—the night he was shot. People asked her if Robert Kennedy would become President and she said—that was rather odd—she said: "I don't see him." And some of those around the table thought it was ridiculous that she said that. And she shut her eyes kind of and said: "I just can't see him . . ." you know. And a lot of them didn't believe it. They thought that she was ignoring him or something. She said: "I can't see Kennedy. He's not clear in my vision," and she kind of halfway shut her eyes and tried to concentrate, to answer them. And they were all very anxious to know about his future.

Afterwards I said to her: "Jeane, it's rather odd. After all he's number one for the Democrats." And she said: "I just can't envision him, really." She said: "I lose him." I know she was upset at that meeting and she wasn't as coherent as she usually is. All these questions asked from the audience and she's not answering them, so it would upset the whole meeting, the whole luncheon, it seemed to disturb the whole thing. There was a kind of a feeling of uneasiness all around.

June Wright resumes her testimony:

That afternoon, after we parted, I stayed in the hotel [Ambassador] and tried to phone Rose Kennedy all afternoon. I've known her for a long time. I first met her in Miami at Elliott Roosevelt's house. She was in the Ambassador Hotel that afternoon with Bobby and the campaign crowd.

I spent about an hour and a half telephoning upstairs to Rose and I couldn't get past her secretary. I kept telling her who I was and how well I knew Mrs. Kennedy, but it still didn't matter. Mrs. Kennedy was very busy, the secretary explained. She said: "We'll check and call you back." I called at least four times and then I stayed at the phone nearly all afternoon.

Well, I just didn't stick it out, that's all. You know, when you live in Miami and you're in Los Angeles on a trip and have friends waiting to take you to Chasen's, you don't fool around that long, that's all.

The night of the assassination [June 4/5] I was in the Holly-wood-Roosevelt Hotel in bed watching television and saw the whole thing happen: when Kennedy came out and addressed his workers and thanked them for all they'd been doing and every-thing and then "Bang!" it went and I was so upset I think I watched television for about ten minutes more before I really got my bearings. And then I grabbed the phone and called Jeane. She was back in Washington and there it was three o'clock in the morning.

I knew I was waking her in the middle of the night, but I felt I had to tell her. She answered the phone rather groggily and I said: "This is June," and I said, "I . . ." And she said: "I know, June. I know *exactly* what happened. You don't have to say any-thing."

I said: "Exactly what you said would happen has happened."

She said: "I know." And that was it.

Brian:
You didn't even tell her what had happened?

Wright:
She knew. She knew exactly.

You were convinced?

Wright:
I knew she knew.

What Mrs. Wright had seen on television was Robert Kennedy lying fatally wounded on the floor of the Ambassador Hotel kitchen, while men struggled and shouted, trying to get the gun from Sirhan Sirhan. Kennedy lay dying, a bullet in his brain, a few feet from where Jeane Dixon had spoken so fearfully of seeing his body rising through the ceiling—just a week before.

In San Francisco, at about one in the morning of June 5, Ira Walsh (see also Chapter 12) heard on a news bulletin, a report of Robert Kennedy's condition by a neurosurgeon. Astonished, Walsh immediately phoned a friend in New York, TV executive Tom Swafford.

Ira Walsh testifies:

The neurosurgeon was talking to one of the NBC people and he said: "If we didn't know that somebody had shot Senator Kennedy, it looks like he could have shot himself, because the wound is in the back of the ear."

I flipped when I heard that, and phoned Tom Swafford. He was in New York. I told him what the neurosurgeon had just said and I asked Tom: "What do you think of that?" And then he remembered what Jeane Dixon had said to us two years before. Tom and I had been having lunch with her then and Jeane suddenly stopped eating and said to us that she had a funny feeling Bobby Kennedy was going to commit suicide. That was two years before he was killed.

Swafford, a CBS television executive, recalls Jeane Dixon's prediction about Robert Kennedy.

Tom Swafford testifies on September 22, 1972:

Jeane told Ira Walsh and me that she couldn't escape the feeling that Robert Kennedy would commit suicide. She said to us: "I keep seeing a pistol behind his ear."

I don't know which of us called the other one first. I had got up at five o'clock that morning, eager to find out how the election in California had gone, and I turned on the television and this whole thing was being played before our eyes. I stood in the living room and the thing was being recounted by Walter Cronkite. I turned cold all over, more with the awareness that Jeane had told us this not all that long before, than at the horror of what had happened at the Ambassador Hotel.

Obviously that was a terrifying experience and it has given television so many problems since then; because kings and princes and emperors and presidents have been assassinated since the beginning of time. But, Goddammit, they've never had a United States Senator die in their living rooms before. It was just a shattering experience for the entire nation, and ever since then every problem we have, they blame television for.

I waited until later in the morning to call Ira—or he called me —I don't know. But we both remembered Jeane's prediction.

16

"You Will Be Married Next Year"
James Fahey Marries

James Fahey:

I had asked Dave Powers to try to get Joan Kennedy to arrange a meeting between the Kennedys and Mrs. Dixon. The next time I saw Dave was about a month after the Bobby Kennedy assassination. He was very sad when he told me that it just slipped his mind because there was so much to do during the trip to Ireland. Then I told him that Jeane Dixon had said that Bobby Kennedy would never become President of the United States and she also predicted his death.

I was talking to Jeane Dixon early in 1969, and she told me I would be married the following year. I was very surprised at the prediction and thought to myself, "But I'm not going with anyone." I had no intention of getting married. I was fifty-one then and almost a confirmed bachelor.

I did know Adele, the widow of a naval commander, but we were just acquaintances. I'd seen her casually with mutual friends. Some weeks after Jeane's prediction, I asked Adele to go out with me; and it was the third time we'd been out together when I sur-

prised myself by asking her to marry me. It was strange. I didn't
plan to ask her; the words just came out of my mouth.

Adele Fahey:

I didn't accept Jim's proposal right away. I had decided that I'd
only marry again if the man were right for me in every way. In
fact, I wanted a sign that it would be right for me to marry Jim.

About three months after Jim's proposal, I was passing the little
chapel at Massachusetts General Hospital; and I had a strong
compulsion to go inside. I went in, and was all alone. The lights
were very dim, the candles were lighted on the altar, and music
was playing. It seemed to me that something was about to take
place—a ceremony perhaps. I just sat there looking up at a beautiful blue stained-glass window above the altar in front. All of a
sudden, it was though I was transferred to another place. It was
like a shift of consciousness, like a flick; and I found myself in a
beautiful sunny field. It was surrounded by trees, like a forest really; and I couldn't see anything through the trees. I was standing
in the center of the field; and as I stood there, all of a sudden I
saw a deer come out of the woods, stand on the edge of the field
and lift his head up and sort of sniff the air as though he was getting his bearings. Then he started coming right over to me. I
thought, "How lovely." He stopped right in front of me and
stretched out his head; and I reached my hand out to touch his
nose, thinking, "what a beautiful animal." Then a voice spoke to
me. Now, this voice was within me and also without—outside. It
sort of filled everything. The voice said to me, "Do you think I
would lead anyone to you who was not true?"

Then all of a sudden, the meaning of it all came to my mind,
and I associated this with Jim. I knew that I had my sign.

Everything faded away then, and I was back there in the little
chapel. Of course, I couldn't wait to tell Jim that I did want to
marry him.

That was in May of 1969, and we were married in July of 1970
in Mettupatti, South India, at the church built from the royalties
of Jim's book. It was the wedding of all weddings with thousands
of people there. Someday we will go back to India with Jeane
Dixon to dedicate our beautiful cathedral to President Kennedy

and to Senator Robert Kennedy, the two brothers whose deaths Jeane Dixon predicted. Jim always says that if only Robert Kennedy had listened to Jeane Dixon, he would be alive today and be President in 1976.

17

"A White Man Will Shoot Governor Wallace"
Her Hairdressers

Michael Konowaluk:

About two weeks before Bobby Kennedy got shot I was saying something about him and Jeane Dixon said: "He's going to be shot, with two bullets in his head." She said it just like it came out of thin air. I didn't question her. I always tease her when it comes out true. I say: "Another lucky guess." But this time it almost hit it right on the head and after it happened I was shocked. Then, with Governor Wallace, we were discussing something about him getting shot and I said: "Oh, God, I hope it doesn't happen." She said: "He's going to be shot." And I said: "Will it be down South?" And she said: "No, north of the Mason-Dixon line." That was about six weeks, maybe more, maybe less, before it happened.

I asked if a black man would shoot him and she said no, it would be a white man. She said it would be terrible, but Wallace would survive. She said it would stay with him a long time. I don't know what that could be interpreted as.

Blase Di Vizio:

As I remember it, it was something to do with the morning

papers. We had just picked up the paper and we were talking about the election, Wallace and all the rest of it. And that's when she said he would be shot. And then she said a white man would do it. I remember asking if Wallace would die, and she said no. [Wallace was shot on May 15, 1972.]

One day we were going out to lunch with her and some woman stopped her on the street. I don't know who the woman was, but she said: "Thank you for telling me not to take that plane, because that plane did go down." That was a year or two ago.

18

Psychiatrist-Magician
Dr. F. Regis Riesenman

To date the closest to a scientific investigation of Jeane Dixon's psychic powers has been undertaken by a psychiatrist who is also a skilled magician, Dr. F. Regis Riesenman.

He is able, as a magician, to distinguish between genuine mind reading and the trick variety in which a code, partner, or electronic equipment is used. As a psychiatrist and neurologist he is trained to spot the deluded—and the sane. So that he is well equipped to tell if Jeane Dixon is hallucinating when she sees visions, and whether her claim that she can read other minds is valid.

Among the many so-called psychics he has met and put to the test over the years he has judged only a small number of them to be genuine; among them Peter Hurkos and Olof Jonsson. What of Jeane Dixon?

Dr. Riesenman had heard of Jeane Dixon's apparent ability to foretell the future and he was eager to meet her, which he did in 1961, when they were guests at a private party.

There, while he was entertaining fellow guests with a mind-reading trick he'd decided to do on the spur of the moment, Jeane

Dixon was in the kitchen with the door closed, out of sight and earshot, apparently helping prepare dinner.

She didn't enter the room, says Dr. Riesenman, until he had finished his trick. Then, he recalls, she walked up to him and whispered that she knew he had been doing a mind-reading trick. This surprised him. How could she possibly know?

She further surprised him by describing how the trick was done.

Dr. Riesenman concluded, after reviewing the possibilities, that there was only one way Jeane Dixon could have known what he was doing while she was shut away in the kitchen. She must, he decided, have read his mind—and that, unlike his own performance, it was no trick.

From that time on his interest in Jeane Dixon remained steady. And fortunately he was able to see her often because she lived close to his home in Arlington, Virginia.

Russian scientist L. L. Vasiliev, a physiologist and pioneer investigator of the paranormal, mocked Professor William James for bothering to study mediums; saying that in his opinion mediums are either emotionally disturbed, or lying.

Dr. Riesenman agrees that many fall into these categories, but that Jeane Dixon is not one of them.

Although he cannot be compared with parapsychologists like Dr. J. B. Rhine or Dr. Gardner Murphy, who favor controlled experiments, Dr. Riesenman has the advantage of observing psychics in their own environment, working spontaneously. He has kept a close watch on Jeane Dixon for thirteen of the fifteen years he has known her.

Brian:

When you worked out the percentage of Jeane Dixon's prophecies that came true, did you take all her published predictions over the years?

Dr. Riesenman:

No, I figured her channels of communication. If I know the channel she used when she gets this thing, it's 100 per cent in certain channels, it's as low as 50 per cent in other channels. The overall run is 70 per cent. [Dr. Riesenman believes Mrs. Dixon has six channels for getting extrasensory information: (1) the highest channel, a direct vision; (2) a brief, indirect vision; (3) an intellectual impression, or intuitive knowledge; (4) by meditation; (5) telepathy; (6) impressions she gets by touching fingertips or just talking with people.] But don't forget that a lot of her predictions she puts in the papers two or three times a year are not really predictions based on ESP. They're predictions based on an intuitive and perceptive knowledge, based on rational inference from knowledge that she gets.

You know that scientists say that the simplest explanation is the likeliest one when mysterious events are involved . . . ?

Dr. Riesenman:
    Right.

You remember when you first met Jeane Dixon and you believed she was capable of reading minds because she knew you were performing a mind-reading act to guests in the living room, despite the fact she was in the kitchen? Couldn't it have been possible that your hostess was in the kitchen with Mrs. Dixon and told her that you did mind-reading tricks at parties?

Dr. Riesenman:
    No, because Mrs. Dixon was alone in the kitchen. She was the only one who was not in the area where I did the trick and she came out before anybody left the room.

[After that first meeting in 1961, Dr. Riesenman didn't see Mrs. Dixon for another two years. Then he called in at her office and showed her a photograph of his family. Among them was his six-year-old daughter, Mary Alice. Mrs. Dixon, says Dr. Riesenman, merely touched the photograph, then mimicked exactly the way his daughter walked, and said that Mary Alice was unable to walk properly—not because of cerebral palsy, which was believed to be the reason, but because her hips were dislocated. Dr. Riesenman afterward discussed this with specialists at the Institute of Health, where Mary Alice had been examined some time before. They said that X-rays taken at that time had indicated that Mary Alice had dislocated hips, but that they had not told Dr. Riesenman of this because they thought he was chiefly concerned with her mental condition.]

When Mrs. Dixon looked at the photo of your daughter, then imitated her awkward walk, isn't it possible that in the two years since she had known you, some mutual friend could have told Mrs. Dixon you had a young daughter who walked awkwardly?

Dr. Riesenman:

That might be possible. But Mrs. Dixon did it in such a way—the same characteristic way that Mary Alice went up and down stairs, and how she moved her left foot. Only a doctor could have explained it to her that way. She saw there was a bilateral dislocation of both hips.

Did Mrs. Dixon use the expression "bilateral dislocation"?

Dr. Riesenman:

She said: "She was born with both hip sockets missing"—which is what I as a doctor would describe as bilateral dislocation.

Do you think that Mrs. Dixon gets revelations from God and that she can perceive things by extrasensory means?

Dr. Riesenman:

There's no question about the extrasensory things. And as far as the revelations are concerned, it seems that a couple of times they were definitely revelations, when she went through cosmic-conscious type experiences.

Are you a Catholic?

Dr. Riesenman:

Yes.

I ask because a number, though not all the people who have been witnesses to Jeane Dixon's powers are Catholics. And it seems to me that people who believe in prayer and God and who have faith, are more open to the extrasensory world.

Dr. Riesenman:

That's true. Any religious person would have a head start on anything like that. All these things are expressions of the soul; the psychological soul manifests itself.

JEANE DIXON ABOUT DR. RIESENMAN
November 27, 1975

Brian:
When you first encountered Dr. Riesenman, he was doing a trick and you picked it up telepathically.

Jeane Dixon:
Yes, I picked up what he was doing. I was in another room.

There was absolutely no indication of what he had been doing, for you to have been able to tell by normal means—like pieces of paper on the floor?

Jeane Dixon:
Nothing. You see, as he was doing it I was doing it. In other words, I was doing it with him. And when I came into the room I told him that and also how the trick was done. When you ask how these things are done, I say telepathically. You see, I'm right there. My channel takes on his channel, and I'm doing just what he's doing.

Do you know all his other thoughts?

Jeane Dixon:
Sometimes you do. But, you see, the way it is you can only have one channel at a time. It's like a radio or television. You cannot pick up two channels.

The question I can imagine people asking is this: Isn't it a trivial thing to be able to pick up telepathically that a man is doing a playful trick?

Jeane Dixon:
I don't think it's quite that trivial. It's quite important, I think.

But compared with when you picked up that Frank Sinatra, Jr., was going to be kidnapped, it was trivial. (Or rather, that someone close to Frank Sinatra would be in danger.)

Jeane Dixon:

I know. But, you see, that's the same thing. They had very strong thoughts. It is no different. It was the strongest channel there and that channel came through to me.

But, don't you agree that with the kidnappers you would have picked up emotional thoughts, and Dr. Riesenman's would have been more lighthearted?

Jeane Dixon:

It doesn't matter whether they're emotional or what they are— the same way as you pick up words on the radio and television.

So you have no way of screening out the less important?

Jeane Dixon:

No. You get the one station that you're tuned into. Now, say something crosses that station, something that's more powerful, it can cut that station out.

Have you literally had hundreds of occasions when you've read people's minds?

Jeane Dixon:

I do that every day.

And when you check up with them, are you nearly always right?

Jeane Dixon:

When I check up with them. But you don't do things like that. You see, Denis, I don't think people understand. That happens to be one of my talents. It's like . . . you take an artist who can paint. You can't sit down and paint all the time unless you sell those pictures. I can't sit down and do this all of the time. I make my money selling real estate. I've got to keep that going.

Did you know Dr. Riesenman's daughter had no hip sockets, just by looking at a photograph of her?

Jeane Dixon:

I saw a photograph of her—but I took on her being. The same way as I took on Dr. Riesenman's being when he was doing those tricks. I am the person at that moment. I'm not myself. I can't tell you what that is . . . I don't know if there is a word to describe that ability. But when it happens, I can feel myself without any hip sockets. I can feel it.

You're doing something that might be akin to hypnosis, perhaps, when you take over the person's personality.

Jeane Dixon:
Yes, it is. Yes.

You not only feel how they are, and how they move, but . . . ?

Jeane Dixon:
They give me their pains and their thoughts and everything.

What's the longest you've ever done that—that it's endured?

Jeane Dixon:
The minute that I get the answer—then I put myself in another channel to try to get the cure.

Is it a strange feeling?

Jeane Dixon:
For me, it isn't strange, it's the natural thing. You see, Denis, people don't understand that. It's the same as an artist when he sees the picture he's painted. It's as natural as natural can be.

19

Voices from the Past: Brothers and Sisters

As Jeane Dixon tells it, her early life was enchanting. Introduced in California to the world of the occult when she was eight, by a gypsy who gave her a crystal ball and predicted that she would be "blessed with the gift of prophecy," young Jeane immediately began making prophecies—that the gypsy was in danger of scalding herself, that Jeane's sister Evelyn (Pinky) would get an airplane for her sixteenth birthday, that her brother Erny Pinckert would be a great athlete—all of which, says Jeane, proved true.

Jeane recalls meeting George Bernard Shaw in Europe and how he said that as well as both being psychic they shared another gift —"the ability to keep a secret."

She shook hands with actress Carole Lombard in a Los Angeles beauty parlor, and warned her, says Jeane, to stay away from airplanes for six weeks. But the blond star ignored the warning and was killed in a plane crash a few days later (in 1942).

The daughter of an indulgent father who retired at forty-five, Jeane resolved to be an actress or a nun. She played Mary Magdalene in *The Life of Christ* at the Hollywood Bowl and a lady-in-waiting in *Midsummer Night's Dream*. But the role she finally chose was to be the wife of James Dixon. She had been in love with him since she was a girl and was heartbroken when he married someone else. Then she found that he was divorced, and despite the fact she was a Catholic and Dixon the son of a Methodist minister, she became his second wife shortly before World War II.

This has been the picture of Jeane Dixon's early life, reflected in the biography *A Gift of Prophecy* and echoed in the dozens of other books that have mentioned her and in the hundreds, if not thousands of articles about her in newspapers and magazines throughout the world.

Was this a reasonably accurate picture of the young Jeane Dixon? Why had there never been any accounts of the young Jeane Dixon by her brothers and sisters? Did they regard their now famous sister as a prophet? Would they confirm or refute the image of a wonder-woman in the making?

I spoke with Jeane Dixon's brother Curt, and three of her sisters, Mrs. Elsie Evans, Mrs. Evelyn (Pinky) Brier, and Mrs. Ella Miller.

But the one perhaps closest to Mrs. Dixon is her brother Erny Pinckert, who lives in California. A former All-American halfback at the University of Southern California, he played for the Washington Redskins. He was retired and sixty-five when I interviewed him on October 25 and October 27, 1973.

Brian:
Jeane was your baby sister.

Erny Pinckert:
That's right. Getting us always in trouble, because she was mother's pet and she would predict things and mother would stop us from doing them. She wasn't too popular with her older brothers and sisters because she would tell mother and stop us from doing things that we wanted to do, because she felt it was wrong. One of my friends was shot in the foot and Jeane had stopped me from going out with him. She turned the alarm off early in the morning. I was going squirrel hunting and I never did get to go with the two fellows. They passed by—because my father was very stern and strict, and they couldn't interrupt, because we used to go out at six in the morning. And then she stopped a

lot of things. She was mother's pet . . . I never believed in that prediction thing, but she hit them pretty good when she was a kid.

When you say your friend was shot in the foot, was the implication that Jeane thought you might have been hurt, too, if you had gone with him?

Pinckert:

Yes. He was crawling under a fence and dragging the gun and it went off. And Jeane said: "That could have been your head or part of your body." She had a bad feeling [before it happened], came in about two-thirty in the morning, and turned the alarm off. And I slept on through till about seven o'clock.

How old were you then?

Pinckert:

I guess I was about sixteen.

When you say your father was strict—would he have stopped you from going on the squirrel hunt?

Pinckert:

No. But my friends would have come and knocked on the door or whistled or something like that to wake me [Jeane having turned off his alarm], but they knew my dad was real tough on those things, so they went on ahead and went on hunting and left me.

Do you recall in A Gift of Prophecy how your sister Jeane predicted you would be a wonderful athlete? Do you remember the occasion when she did that?

Pinckert:

Yes, I remember that.

Could she have predicted it because you were a pretty good athlete, anyway?

Pinckert:

Well, no, I didn't go out for sports until high school; not in grammar school. And Jeane always said: "Why don't you take up one of the sports? You'd be good at it." And she kept urging me, and so when I was in high school I took up football.

According to the account in A Gift of Prophecy . . . *most of you Pinckert children would get cars . . .*

Pinckert:
Yes, when we came of age, you know. My father would let us drive and get us a car.

Do you ever remember Jeane predicting that her sister Evelyn would get—not a car—but a plane?

Pinckert:
Pinky we call her. Yes, I remember that. And I remember when she was taking lessons and Jeane said: "She's going to have her own plane." I said: "That's out of the question." But, by God, she did get her own plane.

I've spoken with your sister Jeane many times and what I feel is, that with people she's very close to, very often she makes astonishing predictions that come true. But when she makes the printed predictions, you know, General de Gaulle is going to do this, and Jackie Kennedy's not going to remarry, and so on; when it's not somebody close to her, it probably doesn't come true. Do you agree with me?

Pinckert:
Yes. I know on the blackout, I believe she predicted that a year before it happened.

You mean the power failure on the East Coast?

Pinckert:
That's right. That was published.

I think she also predicted something for your wife, who was also her best friend.

Pinckert:
Jeane knew her before I did and she arranged for the date and she said: "You'll be settling down and getting married." I didn't believe it at all. I was a confirmed bachelor and I didn't think I'd

ever get married. I played professional football. And by George I
did get married to this girl who was her best friend.

*When she told you you'd be an athlete, and encouraged you—I
think she encourages a lot of people to do things she feels they're
right for, then it's not strictly a prediction so much as she's intuitive and encourages them. Would you agree with me?*

Pinckert:

That's right, she does. She was fairly young then, you know,
when I took up sports. She was about seven and, I guess, in kin-
dergarten.

Did you know the gypsy who, according to A Gift of Prophecy
gave Jeane her first crystal ball?

Pinckert:

No. I don't recall that.

Did you know the Jesuit priest who taught her astrology?

Pinckert:

Oh, yes, I remember some of that. He'd come to our home and
they'd spend time together, in the living room. I never did bother
. . . I was busy. I never did follow through or watch what she was
doing. You see, she and mother were very close.

*Did she make any of her famous predictions to you, like the
JFK or Robert Kennedy assassinations?*

Pinckert:

I talk to her about once a week regularly on the phone. She was
very much concerned about him [JFK] going to Texas, I remember and she said: "I'm so upset about Kennedy going and I've
tried to warn them and they won't listen to me." Evidently the
Kennedys ignored Jeane in a way. They don't like predictions.

When you read A Gift of Prophecy *and* My Life and
Prophecies *did you think them a bit exaggerated, exactly true, or
. . . what did you think of them?*

Pinckert:

Between you and I, I'm not a believer in things like that. I'm not much of a religious person either. I want to see where it is, and now, you know. I'm a believer in everyday life. As for ESP, it doesn't get me. Maybe it's because Jeane was so close to mother and disturbed us kids on different things. She was not liked as much as . . . We loved her, but we got disturbed because of all these different things. If Jeane thought something was wrong . . . and she was just a kid and you're ten years older . . . and she kind of rules everything; it's like a spoiled brat in a way. A lot of our attitude at times was that towards her. But when it came down to it, we loved Jeane. She's a very sweet girl and she was small, and of course we were all older. And if she rules through mother, on her ideas and beliefs, well, you know, it made it pretty rough.

Did your mother have any psychic ability?

Pinckert:

No, she just went with Jeane on things, decisions, you know.

If Jeane gave you a warning, would you follow it?

Pinckert:

I think I would now. Because she predicted I'd lose my wife before she'd be sixty, or around fifty-five. And she said I'd be extremely ill and that I'd just gradually pull through. And I laughed. I was in the forties then. I laughed and I got a kick out of it. I felt great and thought it would never happen. It all happened. I lost my wife. I almost died three times. I was fifty-seven then. Jeane said before I was sixty it would happen. She predicted that ten years before it happened. I thought she was kidding. I'd forgotten all about it. Finally it all came back to me.

Did her warning of these two things help you in any way?

Pinckert:

No, because I ignored them. I felt so great and my wife was wonderful. I never thought she would die of cancer . . . but she did.

But Jeane didn't say "cancer"?

Pinckert:

No, she said: "You're going to lose Mildred and you're going to be extremely ill before you're sixty." And sure enough I was.

How long before you lost your wife did Jeane predict it?

Pinckert:

About nine years. And we were both fine then. We were laughing. We were at a party.

But wasn't it a frightening thing to tell you: if you had believed it?

Pinckert:

Well, it would be. Still, I didn't believe that. And I'd forgotten it over a period of time, until I was reminded of it. My daughter and I remember distinctly where we were, and it was such a fast thing. And Jeane didn't dwell on it. I said: "You're kidding!" I'd never felt so good in my life and I'd retired from football and everything. And Mildred looked great.

What I don't understand is this: You know she said these things and you know they came true, and as a result of that now you follow her advice; but at the same time you say you don't believe it.

Pinckert:

It's awfully hard. Of course there have been just those things that have happened. And, like I say, I was young and she was just a kid. Those things were disturbing. And that's why, maybe, I didn't follow her closely, or believe in the things she predicted; perhaps because with mother and us she was more or less a thorn in the side.

Was your father wealthy?

Pinckert:

He was comfortable. We had everything. He was in the real estate business more or less. He bought property and then he'd sell it.

I spoke again with Jeane's sisters and her brother Curt in October 1973, before getting back to Erny. Having been subjected to the probing questions of Daniel Greene of The National Observer, in which he was trying to pinpoint the age, determine the number of marriages, and establish the truth about the early life

*of their famous sister Jeane Dixon, it's hardly surprising that they
were inclined to be question-shy. This is what they said:*

. . . Mother and Dad always had money in the bank and they
were well-to-do. We had the largest dairy . . . and we always had
more than any of the other kids I played with. . . . Jeane was the
sweetest girl. Her nickname was Honey. She never caused any
trouble. She was just wonderful. She was a nice girl. She still is.

. . . I didn't know that she married a Charles Zuercher. I have
a cousin called Lydia who looked a little like Jeane.

. . . Listen, I'm not going to say too much around here. I always get in trouble.

. . . Jeane was always different when she was a girl growing
up. She was by herself, and next to my mother always. She never
ran around . . . She was always a very, very nice girl. She was
very quiet and had a wonderful personality. Everybody was after
her and she'd always run out and hide. She was shy.

. . . My goodness, Jeane has done more for people than anybody I ever heard of. And I get a little upset with busybodies. If I
had the time I'd like to do a story on these people that write these
stories. [Laughs] I think we need heroes. I don't think we should
tear people apart . . . I don't interfere with Jeane's life one way or
another. If she told me she was sixteen, that's all right with me. I
couldn't care less. It's not that important.

. . . My brothers and sisters are great. I have one that's a dentist. I have an electrical engineer . . . all of them are great in their
own line. You know, you are born with your relatives, you choose
your friends. And I'm very fortunate in having wonderful brothers
and sisters.

. . . Jeane is great and she gives of her whole life to people.

20

The Investigative Reporter Nothing at Face Value

When I heard that Daniel St. Albin Greene, an investigative reporter for *The National Observer*, was zeroing in on Jeane Dixon, I interviewed him, then sent him the transcript. He returned it on January 4, 1974, writing, in part: "I have edited the transcript to make my answers more articulate and to be fair to the people I am discussing. Some sections I have excised because the comments are either too vague or potentially libelous. And I have added some responses to update or support my views of the facts I've cited."

I have also edited the transcript in the same way and for the same reasons.

Greene:

It started off to be just a biography of Jeane, and I simply set out to develop her life story, apart from the various books that have been printed. I read the books, and then it dawned on me that they were largely written just from her information translated by ghost writers. I talked to Ruth Montgomery and Rene Noorbergen, and I found out from them that they had not really done any independent research; they had simply taken her story as she told it, and written it, and now they're sorry they did. So I just did the job, and I found some things that haven't been printed before, which Mrs. Dixon now denies.

I've interviewed Jeane a lot, and I interviewed many relatives and friends. I touched about every base I could think of . . . I didn't spend a lot of time interviewing her employees. I interviewed a few of them, and I finally decided that nobody in her employ was going to be terribly candid with me.

I certainly did not enter into this project with any desire to muckrake. I entered into it, as you did, with a completely objective point of view. I wanted to see if there was any compelling, persuasive evidence that she had done these things, and my conclusion was that there is not. I talked with person after person, at some length, and we discussed these famous cases of prognostication. And to be perfectly frank, I haven't found a completely reliable witness—a person who is reputable, intelligent, and rational, and who really wouldn't have any reason to corroborate what she said.

I spent two weeks trying to prove or disprove the story of the visits to Franklin Roosevelt.

I contacted the Roosevelt Library; I talked to Roosevelt's children; I talked to Jim Bishop, who's doing a book on Roosevelt's last year; I spent a great deal of money and time, and I asked each person: "Is there any way to prove that Jeane Dixon ever visited the President in his office and made these predictions?" I've not come up with anybody who could do it, have you? [See Estelle Friedrichs' account, Chapter 5 and Chapter 25.]

Brian:

I was incredibly impressed by Jean Stout's account of how Mrs. Dixon predicted the three astronauts would be burned to death. Not only is Jean Stout emphatic that Jeane Dixon predicted it, but Mrs. Stout said she kept a journal, to which she refers, and there's no working-for-her tie-up at all.

Greene:

Mrs. Stout is one of Mrs. Dixon's most loyal friends in Washington.

The weight of the JFK and the Robert Kennedy predictions is astonishing when you speak to several people, all of whom say things like: "I was driving in a car with Mrs. Dixon. She was driving unusually slowly and said: 'I'm terrified it's going to happen in a day or two!' and shortly before the assassination: 'Mrs. Dixon asked me to warn the White House.' Three days before the Bobby Kennedy assassination, Mrs. Dixon is in the same hotel and says to the woman next to her: 'I see his body going through the ceiling.'"

Greene:

Who is that woman?

June Wright.

Greene:

I talked to her: a long-time friend of Jeane's who believes in psychic phenomena. I've interviewed a number of people Mrs. Dixon cites as witnesses to that Robert Kennedy prophecy. Not one of them I talked to was willing to back up what she said, except the Florida friend [June Wright], who couldn't qualify as an impartial witness. People who could not really be linked to this world of psychic phenomena, such as Senator Tower's wife, the woman who was her host in Texas, people who were in Miami with her when she was supposed to have blurted out the Bobby Kennedy prophecy during that Kentucky Fried Chicken Convention—none of these people are now willing to verify what she said in the book. I talked to the man she quotes on two or three occasions, who later worked in her foundation with her.

I know: he's a disgruntled ex-employee.

Greene:

He was on the board of directors of Children to Children. He claims now he did not hear the things she said. I interviewed two people who were with her in Texas when Jeane Dixon was supposed to have said that Bobby was going to die, including Mrs. John Tower. Neither of them is willing to corroborate, now, what she said in the book.

Did you contact Kay Halle?

Greene:

Yes, and I found her rather persuasive. But since then, I've talked to other people, not only people who worked for Mrs.

Dixon but also people who know some of the people in High Society that Mrs. Dixon keeps quoting. And they say that Kay is not an impartial witness. In my manuscript I said that the John Kennedy [assassination] prediction was impressive to me. I couldn't break it. Of all the things I investigated, this did stand up as a fairly provocative accomplishment. I'm the first to admit that there are weird things happening in this world that we can't explain, and this may be one of them. But one viable prediction over a thirty-year career certainly does not make somebody a prophet, a God-given messenger.

Did you speak with Ivy Baker Priest, the former U.S. treasurer?

Greene:
No, I did not.

She will tell you, for example, that Jeane Dixon predicted in 1947 or 1948 that Nixon would be President.

Greene:
I wonder how many other Republican congressmen have heard her say the same about them.

She's stuck with Nixon through thick and thin . . . Of course the difficulty is with so many of these predictions which she says are based on telepathy—knowing what people are thinking at a certain time—people's minds change.

Greene:
But to the rationalist this is the classic cop-out—another way of saying: "If I'm wrong, there's a reason." I played this game of trying to prove or disprove predictions for some time. I devoted most of my time to biography. But I did devote a few weeks to just playing this game of calling up witnesses and saying: "Do you remember this?" and so forth. The general lesson I learned from this—and I finally just got tired of playing the game and decided, well, this is the way it is—was that on every single prediction, I could get, say, one person who said "yes" and one person who said "no," sometimes two people who said "yes" and two people who said "no," and so forth. I could never get unanimous agreement. I got vague recollections, disagreements on exactly what was said, and sometimes absolute contradictions.

Did you get to H. L. Hunt?

Greene:
No, but I quoted something of yours saying he'd made a lot of money on her predictions.

You didn't cover Jeane Dixon correctly predicting the Kentucky Derby winner to Hunt and others?

Greene:
I did research that horse race she describes in one of her books, when she predicted a winner at Bowie. I talked to some of the people who were with her there, and they don't remember it as the mystical phenomenon she describes. They remember that Jeane Dixon looked over the program and said: "I feel Summer Sunshine's going to win," and put two dollars on it. And it won. They remember simply that Jeane Dixon played a hunch and won.

There's one remarkable prediction I investigated recently about Jeane Dixon warning her husband not to catch a plane. Did you follow that up?

Greene:
I really didn't know how I could follow it up. There's only one witness.

And he's surfaced after twenty-five years.

Greene:
A witness other than her husband?

Right.

Greene:
I must admit I'm a skeptical observer, but I have a wide-open mind. I've done a number of articles about the occult. I did a piece on Satanism, and I've done astrology, witchcraft, and psychic mediumship; and in each of these areas I've gone into—because I have a rather expansive mind and I'm willing to believe—I wanted very much to be shown something.

Eileen Garrett was pretty convincing, wasn't she? [Eileen Garrett, founder and president of the Parapsychology Foundation, impressed, among others, J. B. Rhine and Gardner Murphy, with her psychic abilities. She encouraged scientists to study her and other psychics.]

Greene:

Yes. I interviewed Eileen Garrett, and she was a very impressive woman. I think I was the last person to interview Arthur Ford for a national publication. I liked him, but he didn't show me anything that was impressive; because he was an old man by that time . . . I've been to séances and everything . . . I'm a rationalist. But I'm also a person with a very curious mind, and I would love to be shown something that I could write about and say: "Readers, I'm the most skeptical person in the world, but this has impressed *me*." But a person like this, doing an article about Jeane Dixon or any other psychic, is confronted by the same frustration over and over again. He's confronted by statements that might be substantiated by some old man or woman who remembered it thirty years ago. And, damn it, that won't stand up to rational judgment. A person comes to me and says: "Mr. Greene, I just want to verify a statement that Jeane Dixon made in her book because twenty years ago I heard her say that." And I look at this man, and he is sixty-five years old, and I say: "Mr. So and So, do you believe in psychic phenomena?" And he says: "Oh, yes; let me tell you about things that have happened to me."

Now I'm not saying that this proves he's a liar. What I'm saying is that, in any court in the land, he would be considered a prejudiced witness. What I searched for were witnesses about whom I could say: "Okay, if this person substantiates it, I will believe it, because I know this person to be a believable witness." I *can't* find that kind of witness. I interviewed Ruth Montgomery. I said, "Ruth, you're in my business, and you've done the Washington scene as a reporter, and we can talk the same language. Now, look, did it happen this way?" And Ruth tells me: "I look back on it now, and realize there was nothing much that Jeane ever told me that I could prove." And she told me, quite frankly, she's sorry she did the book.

I interviewed Rene Noorbergen. Now, I know Rene's been doing other books on psychic phenomena, but I said: "We talk the same language, and we're in the same business. What d'you think of Jeane Dixon?" He said essentially the same thing Ruth Montgomery said. He is convinced Jeane is inspired by the devil, he told me.

But isn't Noorbergen rather disgruntled?

Greene:
Most of the former associates I interviewed are disgruntled.

But don't you find Ruth Montgomery an unreliable witness, when she prefaces her first book on Jeane Dixon by saying the psychic field was completely unknown to her before she did the book, and then she comes out with another book, saying she's been doing automatic writing practically all her life?

Greene:
What Ruth told me was that she was vaguely interested in psychic phenomena when she first met Jeane. But in doing the book with Jeane she became somewhat interested and started doing things herself, and at that point she became a very active and interested student of psychic phenomena, and became convinced that she herself was able to do automatic writing. So she claims it started with Jeane, and since then she has developed powers of her own.

How do you react to Jeane Dixon's prediction printed in the Washington *News in 1968, in which she said Nixon would be involved in a major wiretap scandal?*

Greene:
When wiretaps become news, when people are talking about wiretaps, naturally any psychic's going to come out and say this or that important figure is going to be involved in a wiretap scandal within the next four years.

She specifically named Richard Nixon.

Greene:
Now, you know, for the last six or seven years wiretapping has been a controversial subject. Now, for a politically conservative person, who lives in Washington and makes conservative predic-

tions, it was a fairly logical thing to say. Once again, this is a skeptical attitude. Milbourne Christopher [head of the Occult Investigation Committee of the Society of Magicians, and author of *ESP, Seers & Psychics,* 1970] made a statement to me that makes sense. He said: "If you want to set yourself up as a psychic, and have the gall to do it, and the temperament—as much as you know about the Washington scene, about national and international events—you could, four times a year, release fifty predictions; and you're bound to hit on a fair percentage of them. You might hit on 25 or 30 per cent."

Jeane doesn't do that well. I've been through her published predictions—and you eliminate a great percentage of them that just can't be answered one way or another.

But what I find extraordinary about Jeane Dixon are her spontaneous predictions; the times, for example, when she grips someone's elbow and says: "Keep away from fire!" or, "I can see her burning!" or something like that; and a tragic fire does take place not long afterward. I find that extraordinary.

Greene:

I wish I could find one witness who was just like me, an absolute skeptic who doesn't believe in any of that stuff and who could tell me: "You know, Dan, I don't believe in any of that nonsense, but this woman said that to me."

The Hearst Executive, Ira Walsh, did say that—even now he says: "I don't really believe it—but it happened."

Greene:

This doesn't ring a bell with me. [Ira Walsh incident, Chapter 12.] I'll look over that material and see what I think of it. I would say this. If I ever did a book about Jeane, it would be absolutely objective. It would be a real hard-nosed reporting job, putting every claim to the most merciless examination. I would like to see a book done like that on her. If you really did want to do that kind of book, I would be willing to lay some of the material I have in front of you.

It's not going to be merciless, but, in fact, I want to use what you're telling me now, this interview.

Greene:

The material I've got, in my opinion, at this point, is absolutely uncontradictable. I dig up the records, I tape almost all my interviews. When I do a story like this, I'll go to court with it; it's not going to be broken down. The bulk of my file is documentation.

I'm willing to leave this question of whether Jeane Dixon is psychic or not, to the reader's opinion.

I've reached the conclusion that there is no way in the world any of us will ever prove or disprove whether Jeane Dixon is a psychic or not, but there are some parts of her life that can be proved or disproved, by hard documentation, statistics, facts, and figures.

I'm doing exactly that; I'm leaving it up to the reader. I'm objective and open-minded, but I'm inclined to believe there's something in it, and I'm impressed with two or three of the witnesses and I'm very impressed with the considerable evidence of her JFK and Robert Kennedy predictions. How did you find Jeane Dixon's brothers and sisters? Were they positive, negative, or neutral?

Greene:

They're not close to her; as one sister told me: "They're money people; I'm not money people." She was referring to Erny and Evelyn and Jeane, who are the prominent figures in the family. The rest of them very seldom talk to Jeane; they have not known her well for decades; she came East, they stayed West; they don't correspond much. There's a great difference in ages, cultures, and life-style.

When I first interviewed her brothers and sisters, they were cooperative and cordial. Erny was very vague about details; but Curt, Elsie Evans, and Ella Miller were very knowledgeable about the early years and gave me most of the information about Jeane's childhood, when everybody knew her as Lydia. They helped me develop the chronology of births for all the Pinckert children, and later I found Wisconsin birth records that verified this chronology. Curt, Elsie Evans, Ella Miller, and Erny Miller all agreed with the records—that Lydia Pinckert was born January 5, 1904.

But before my article was published [in *The National Observer* on October 27, 1973], Jeane got Curt, Emy, Elsie, and Ella to send telegrams to *The Observer* saying that Jeane was born January 5, 1918, and had only been married once.* I subsequently talked to Curt by phone, and he again verified that Jeane was born in 1904, and said he knew nothing about the telegrams. So make your own judgment about the veracity of the Pinckert family.

I've heard from people who worked with Jeane Dixon for years. They say she has a magnificent capacity to convince people. And they were convinced by her until so much happened that the other side of her story just finally became compelling, and they said: "Look, this woman is doing more harm than good."

I personally like Jeane Dixon. But the last time we met I said to her: "I would be the happiest person in the world if I could write an article that you would love. But when I went into this, I told you I was going into it as a hard-nosed, investigative reporter; that I wasn't going to take anything at face value, that I was going to look for evidence in the same way I did for the biographical pieces I did on Spiro Agnew and Lady Bird Johnson and a number of others. I don't know what I'm going to find. We'll just have to wait and see."

And when I had finished it, I told her exactly what I said I was going to do, "and please do believe me—that I did it in the most honest way I could do."

* Greene says he has documentary evidence that Jeane Dixon had been married before she married James Dixon. Her first husband, Greene believes, was a Swiss immigrant, Charles Zuercher, and their marriage was in 1928.

21

Jeane Dixon Herself: Four Interviews

THE FIRST: JANUARY 14, 1972

On December 7, 1971, McGraw-Hill announced the forthcoming publication of Howard Hughes's autobiography as told to Clifford Irving. Exactly a month later, the disembodied voice of Hughes was heard by seven newsmen in a Los Angeles hotel room. Hughes spoke to them by conference phone from his hotel room in Paradise Island, Nassau. To make sure it was in fact the reclusive billionaire, the veteran newsmen who knew Hughes when he was a man-about-town, asked the voice six test questions. He failed on four of them. Despite that, all seven men were convinced after hearing him talk for half an hour, that he was the genuine article, breaking his fourteen-year silence to say that the McGraw-Hill autobiography was a hoax, and that he had never even met its middleman, Clifford Irving.

McGraw-Hill struck back three days later, on January 10, when Harold McGraw, chairman of the book company, displayed for the press and TV cameras two checks apparently countersigned by Hughes.

Mike Wallace taped on January 13 an exclusive interview with

Irving on CBS's "Sixty Minutes"—which I watched when it was screened three days later. Irving came across to me as completely honest. Wallace, who had some reservations, believed the Hughes autobiography to be genuine. My interview with Jeane Dixon was at the height of the mystery and it wasn't until Irving made the February 14, 1972, cover of *Time* as "Con Man of the Year," that the hoax was revealed.

Brian:
What is your response to the Howard Hughes controversy about his alleged autobiography?

Jeane Dixon:
It is not his. The facts that are written about him may be the facts, but the book is not his doing. I'm sure he hasn't dictated it to this man [Clifford Irving]. But I do not think Hughes will be successful in stopping it. He'll probably have a representative in court to try to stop it, but he won't appear personally.

Do you think Howard Hughes will ever come out of hiding?

Jeane Dixon:
This is what I believe: That when Howard Hughes comes out of hiding, he won't be really out in public. But I think the facts and everything will be known.

Do you think his real reason for hiding is to avoid legal cases?

Jeane Dixon:
I can understand him when he's been hiding like that. You do not know the pressure that the public puts on you when they think you can donate money. I think he's hiding, more or less, to have some privacy. And I can understand it. I wish I had enough money so that I could do the same thing and do my writing and things like that.

Has Hughes still got a big future?

Jeane Dixon:
I think his best works have yet to come. It's going to be in the humanities—not like helping poor people, but helping so that

people will understand themselves better, and so people can be more healthy. The fields of medicine and psychology could be part of the work in which he'll be involved.

Do you think he'll ever marry again?

Jeane Dixon:
No, I don't; not in the foreseeable future.

Are you getting this from telepathy?

Jeane Dixon:
I'm picking up his thoughts.

Why do you think Clifford Irving wrote the book purporting to be Howard Hughes's autobiography? Do you think Irving thought he could get away with it?

Jeane Dixon:
No, no. I think that he's got a lot of the facts there. I think he's got a lot of the facts from people around Hughes. And I think he's got a lot of true facts.

But Irving says he thought he was actually speaking with Howard Hughes. Do you think Irving has been deceived?

Jeane Dixon:
I think probably Irving thought he was talking with Hughes and there could be a misunderstanding. Because people call here [at Mrs. Dixon's office] and swear they've talked with me and they haven't. They've talked with one of my secretaries.

But Irving says he met Hughes in cars . . .

Jeane Dixon:
But people have said they've met me and they've been sitting in the back seat of a car with me and making notes and things like that. They've met me in cars, too, and I won't even remember them. They'll meet me at an airport and bring someone along. I'll be sitting in the front seat and they'll be sitting in the back seat and pretty soon I'll be reading a newspaper article about me and I wouldn't even know the name of the writer. They met me because they were riding in the same car with me and they picked

up a few sentences I spoke. And that's what I believe happened here. I don't believe Clifford Irving is dishonest. He probably was riding in these cars and probably did hear Hughes say these things.

Do you think the book on Howard Hughes will be successful?

Jeane Dixon:
Yes, but I don't think it will be a runaway best seller.

What's your feeling about life on other planets?

Jeane Dixon:
I do not believe there is any life as we know it here, on other planets; maybe some vegetation. When they say people are trying to contact us from other planets, I believe that we're surrounded by holy immortals that give us abounding blessing. I think there are spirits around us, yes, who are probably contacting us, but I do not believe they're from other planets.

Will Ethel Kennedy remarry soon?

Jeane Dixon:
Not right away.

Somebody else is forecasting that she'll marry a man with initials A.W. but that it won't be Andy Williams. Do you go along with that?

Jeane Dixon:
No. But it's a man she knows now and he'll be in some profession. It could be a medical doctor. And I think she'll be happy.

Will Rose Kennedy's autobiography [which she's now writing] be very interesting?

Jeane Dixon:
Terribly interesting, yes. I'm a great admirer of Rose Kennedy. I think the book will help people to have more faith in their Creator.

Sinatra?

Jeane Dixon:
He's still in danger of losing his money and I still believe he

will go into work of a religious nature. That danger of losing his money will follow him around all the days of his life.

Your reaction to the Pentagon Papers?

Jeane Dixon:

It was no surprise to me. That was the context of my speeches from the year 1964. So the information in them was no surprise to me. It was a *surprise* that the Pentagon Papers were stolen and then published like that. You'll remember in 1971 I said: "This is the year that many truths will come out which heretofore have been covered." So, you see, I expected something.

Do you agree that the Pentagon Papers revealed that some politicians were misleading the public?

Jeane Dixon:

I don't think they misled the public. They just didn't *tell* the public. They thought it wasn't important, I guess, to tell the public. But I think it's important.

One of the latest political controversies brought to light by columnist Jack Anderson is about Henry Kissinger and the Indian-Pakistan War. Do you think there will be similar controversies brought to light soon?

Jeane Dixon:

I do and I think they'll go back, even farther back than the Kennedy administration. And of course the mystery of President Kennedy's assassination, the facts about that will be known some day, too. It was a plot. And Oswald was one of the members of the plot. In the November *Reader's Digest* there's an article about how Mexico was almost overthrown. And the spies that were in that, the Communists who were in the Russian Embassy; those were some of the names that I got of people whom Oswald was in contact with.

Will telepathy ever be accepted as a fact by scientists?

Jeane Dixon:

I don't think it will ever be 100 per cent scientifically accepted: I'll tell you why. Because, and I know this to be a fact in my work. Say that I was trying to reach you telepathically. And there is someone who has a stronger "receiving set" than you have. And there'll be interference there. You'll never get it. Because when I pick up thoughts, sometimes I do not think it's the person who's trying to send me a message: I'll pick up the thoughts of someone else whose thoughts are much, much stronger. And everyone does not have the talent to receive and give. They're not born that way. We have many, many piano players, but there's only one Van Cliburn and one Byron Janis. There are only certain people gifted with this talent [telepathy]. And then, too, there can be interference. I would not want to depend upon it. I depend on it when I pick up channels of destiny—because that is the will of God for us as individuals. But when free thought comes in here, and man changes his plans, then you cannot depend on that.

Will life after death ever be proven?

Jeane Dixon:
My recent book *Reincarnation and Prayers to Live By* will tell you about life after death, it tells you exactly what happens to the spirit, it tells you exactly what happens to the soul, it tells you what happens to the body. And that's what I believe in.

Do you see any medical breakthroughs?

Jeane Dixon:
Yes, I see a great medical breakthrough in cancer.

The late Arthur Ford, a spirit medium when he was alive, was believed to have helped bring back the spirit of Bishop Pike's dead son. Do you believe Ford was gifted in this way?

Jeane Dixon:
Yes, I do. I really believe that there are spirits all around us. And I believe that when you contact these—and of course the subconscious mind comes into play, too—but the danger lies where you may have evil spirits come through, directly or indirectly, and bring tragedy and heartaches into your life.

Have you had a vision recently?

Jeane Dixon:
Yes, and it's in my new book *The Call to Glory: Jeane Dixon*

Speaks of Jesus. And there is a vision that affects the whole wide world. Read the epilogue of the book, the last four pages. It's a beautiful, beautiful vision. It's a vision of Jesus, and what he tells us.

Has any interviewer who interviewed you especially impressed you?

Jeane Dixon:

Yes, Mike Douglas. I like him very, very much. Mike Douglas seems to have a channel to the Creator, the Lord. And I admire Douglas a great deal. That doesn't mean I don't admire the other interviewers. But I believe Mike Douglas has much to offer the world—other than in his job as an interviewer. I picked his vibrations up as someone who innately is a very fine, good person.

You feel close kinship with Martha Mitchell, I understand.

Jeane Dixon:

Yes, as far as the press is concerned. Because there are times that I'm misunderstood and others when I'm completely ignored. I have read things in newspapers about me that were so farfetched that I couldn't imagine. And the misquotes about me are something fantastic. She's had the same problems. As a rule I don't bother to correct them because if they do retract the misquotes, where do they put them? They put them back with the funny pages.

How do you explain your statement that Golda Meir is "one of the greatest women that has ever lived. She has the vibrations of Abraham Lincoln"?

Jeane Dixon:

It's a reincarnation of the spirit.

When will there be peace between Israel and the Arab countries?

Jeane Dixon:

There will be divine intervention. I don't want to say exactly when because the Bible says that the Lord is not telling us. But it will be within the foreseeable future and not much more than twenty years from now. Read the last chapter of my book. It tells you all kinds of things.

Is there a quality you most like in people?

Jeane Dixon:

You know the quality I like in other people, and I love this quality, it is faith.

What do you believe is your best quality?

Jeane Dixon:

Love. And I believe my purpose and my mission is this, and I believe it with all my heart: to let people know how great they really are and that they have greatness in themselves if they just work to be themselves and not try to mimic anyone else. I believe I am here to show the people the light of God within themselves.

What is your biggest fault?

Jeane Dixon:

One of my big bad faults is that I try to do too much.

What makes you cry?

Jeane Dixon:

I pray and cry for our country. I pray and I cry for the poor. I even pray and cry for our enemies. I truly, truly do. And then I will sit back sometimes and I will see these people who are abusing their physical bodies by drinking too much and not taking advantage of what God has given them. I walk down the street with tears running down my cheeks thinking about them, seeing them, and wondering why, why, why?

What makes you laugh?

Jeane Dixon:

When I see a child that's well and happy. And when I see someone develop their divinely granted talents to the utmost— and using that to help another.

If you were a dictator, if you were very powerful now, what would you do?

Jeane Dixon:

They wouldn't like me at all, I can tell you that. I would make everybody learn what love is, and that is work, and to develop their talents. I would try to help someone to give them a little inkling of why they were born. I would say: "Let's make it our mission to work for the benefit of one another"—but I'd still let them have a right to their own opinion.

If Jesus Christ appeared in the room with you now, what question would you ask Him?

Jeane Dixon:

I'd say: "Guide me and help me to do *Your* will—let *Your* will be done."

Is there any question you'd ask Him, anything you are curious about?

Jeane Dixon:

No. All I want to do, is do His will for me.

Have you ever thought you were just about to die?

Jeane Dixon:

Once, when I was drowning, a number of years ago. I wasn't frightened at all. Now, isn't that terrible? But I have a peace within myself that I can't describe. But I get upset. I can't keep my promises [to reply to the thousands of letters] and I can't do as much as I want to do. There aren't enough hours to work. Why can't we have twenty hours a day to work?

What makes you angry?

Jeane Dixon:

When I can't keep my promises. It goes back to that again. And I get angry when people do not understand that they've got a mission upon this earth and how great and how peaceful they could be and the love and the life they could have. I get just downright mad when I see people abusing themselves. And I get upset at myself because I don't accomplish as much as I should accomplish. You called me a dozen times before I got together with you. That's what gets me upset.

I understood you were busy.

Jeane Dixon:
I know, but it upsets me.

You were saved from drowning or you saved yourself?

Jeane Dixon:
No, the Lord saved me. I was carried out in Santa Monica, California; carried out in a high, high wave. And it seemed as though the wave just brought me back in and dropped me down on the beach. And when I came to, there I was. I was about nineteen.

Could you briefly give me a typical day in your life? Today for instance?

Jeane Dixon:
This morning I got up at five-thirty. Sometimes I need the alarm clock but I didn't need it this morning. I went downstairs and let the dog out. Then I went into the kitchen. I have what you call a vegetable juice squeezer. And I squeezed some carrot juice, celery juice, and put a little bit of parsley in there. I took a glass of that, along with a vitamin C tablet, to my husband. After that I took a shower, got dressed, and went down to St. Matthew's. Got there at ten minutes to seven. Then after that, from there I went to Schultz's cafeteria and had breakfast. I came to the office at twenty minutes of eight and I've been working and working at the office and trying to get to Denis to talk with him. I had a luncheon appointment with Ira Walsh, whose life I saved. He's here from California. I had to cut that short in order to go on to another appointment and then I've been to the dentist. He gave me a bit of novocaine and here I am trying to talk with you intelligently.

Another day, like yesterday, you would have been lecturing?

Jeane Dixon:
Yesterday I was trying to get back to Washington and there was rainy weather and we circled over the National Airport, had a deuce of a time landing. I had been to Salem, West Virginia, at their college and I was greatly impressed with Professor Hurley

and the children down there were so enthusiastic—there were only 1,500 of them. This seems to be a very wholesome college and they seem to all have a purpose.

When you finish work normally at five-thirty . . .

Jeane Dixon:
Better make it six-thirty . . . Then I go home to dinner. I have a housekeeper who cooks the meals for me and my husband. If I'm lucky enough I get to watch the news, Walter Cronkite. I know him personally and I know his wife. I like him very much. But I don't get to do that always. That's what I call a luxury. After that I take a nap, sleep maybe round to ten, eleven, twelve o'clock, then get up and work on writing my book and on my astrology column. Then I go to bed about one or two. Then I have a little over three hours more sleep—a total of about six.

Does your husband still put a rose on your pillow?

Jeane Dixon:
Every night.

Was there one point in your life you regard as very important?

Jeane Dixon:
It was when I realized that there was a power greater than I and that if I stayed with this, regardless of public opinion, it would carry me on. And I realized that only, I believe, one night when I was in prayer after reading some untruths about me in the newspaper. And this light came to me very clearly, to continue the work that I was doing; the Lord said that he would see it through. That was like a vision, and was maybe about two years ago.

Was that concerning the accusations about money?

Jeane Dixon:
It was when people lied about me and said that I was using money [from her charity Children to Children] to write my books —and trying to discredit me. I was shown the light there, and I was shown the way, and the Lord has encouraged me to continue on with what I'm doing. Because I asked His guidance and it's

s will that I want to do, and *nothing* else but His will. And if I
o that, then I won't hurt people, will I?

Are your visions and revelations, the same thing?

Jeane Dixon:

No. A revelation is the will of God and the will of humanity
cannot change the will of God. Of course, human plans are not always in accord with God's plans, but God alone is great enough
to build good out of what appears to us to be tragic and evil.

Now, this is a revelation: say that God was preparing you for
a revelation. A revelation has nothing to do with a vision. A revelation has nothing to do with any talent. It is His grace and His
power that He works through a human being, for the benefit of
others. And it is always international, for all mankind. Never for
one individual.

All right. Say He's preparing me for a revelation and perhaps
will start tonight. Tomorrow morning I will get up. The world
will not seem like it is to me this morning, or yesterday. I would
get up, and I would be looking at the world through rose-colored
glasses. I would be, it seems, on a higher plateau of Grace. No one
could provoke an argument with me. I'd have no appetite. It
doesn't matter if I eat or not.

And I would be listening to you, but my mind would not be
with you. I would answer you, yet you would feel I was not with
you. Then, as I got to church in the morning and pray, there's
something that holds me, something that holds me all to itself.

I see people around me: they're there and yet they're not there.
But they're there: you see them.

The people who saw me while I had those two revelations in
Washington have said: "I know you're in a trance." But it's not a
trance. They're there and yet they're not.

And then, the fourth day, it's revealed to me. The *fourth* day.
Not the first, second, or third.

Of course, the first time a revelation is given to you, you do not
understand. But you live with it. But the second time, you expect
it and thank God for it.

It's revealed as clearly as we are here now. It's a human being
right there. You see it. You hear it. You live it.

And then you live it for four more days.

The eighth day, here you are again. And you think: "Why can't I always live like that?" But you can't recreate it. You don't even pray for it. You can only prepare for it, because you know it's in God's providence, not yours. I know these things. I just *know* them.

Now, a vision is something else. A vision could come to me in a dream, a vision could come to me at three or four o'clock in the morning. A vision could come at midnight. But that vision can be changed—by fervent prayer and by doing God's will upon this earth as He wants it done. And a vision is not a psychic talent, either. That's given to you.

But when, after four days, you have a revelation, isn't that in the form of a vision?

Jeane Dixon:

It's real life. It's like an act in real life. It isn't like a television show. Remember the assassination of President Kennedy? Now, I was kneeling there in front of the Holy Mother [in St. Matthew's Cathedral]. Now, the statue did not turn to life. But life was there, in all its dimensions.

And here's the funniest thing. When I looked around the church, it was filled, but the seats were empty. And the people were from all over the world, wearing babushkas and everything. I *knew* the church was empty, but I *saw* the people there. And I knew they were the people of the world. Because a revelation is always for everyone.

The revelation of the Anti-Christ is for everyone. And right after that comes divine intervention in Jerusalem. And that's a revelation I haven't told yet. That revelation happened at St. Pat's in New York. That has yet to come. People are not ready for it yet.

How many revelations have you had?

Jeane Dixon:

About seven. I haven't told them all. [They include the JFK assassination, the ecumenical council, and the coming of the Anti-Christ.]

How many visions have you had?

Jeane Dixon:

Visions come quite frequently; of God's plans for people. And if they would only listen when I tell them: "Please don't do that. Like Jimmy [her husband] and the airplane. That was a vision, the airplane crashing. "Don't go, Jimmy! Don't go!" I "saw" the whole thing. And he didn't go. Another man was going to fly on that plane but he didn't go either. He heard a voice warning him not to. So, if your mind is open to the Lord, He will protect you. You have to have this open mind.

Remember, there's the Holy Spirit. That doesn't belong to you: it belongs to the Trinity. And that is a channel I can pick up sometimes. The eternal spirit comes from there and returns to there.

But free will is what takes you through life and you can use it for good or for bad. Now, I'd love you to put this in your book, too: our lives are programmed when we are conceived.

Doesn't that contradict "free will"?

Jeane Dixon:

No, it doesn't contradict free will. Your free will is there. Because, do you remember in the newspapers in 1949 that I said Nixon would be a President of the United States one day—regardless of free will? That was his destiny. That was it.

How shall I put it? We will never change the destiny that was preordained or programmed for us. Free will cannot do that.

Free will can change things in our lives and make our lives different. And when people say—that was their destiny—no, it wasn't their destiny. Free will changes many things in your life. We all have our entrances and exits. Our entrances are preordained, but some are not; they're brought on by our free will, our decisions.

But, if there is in the program of our life, a destiny that is the Lord's destiny for us, we don't change that, even with our free will.

We may go around Robin Hood's barn and a thousand other places, but we'll *end up* there, if it's God's will for us.

Because the will of humanity does not change the will of God.

SECOND INTERVIEW: JEANE DIXON ANSWERS MY QUESTIONS

My chance came to talk with Jeane Dixon at length and in person when she flew to Florida to take part in a charity show on March 23, 1973. I met her at West Palm Beach Airport, drove with her in a cab to the Breakers Hotel—questioning her and taping the interview all the way—and continued the questions for another two hours in the hotel.

I wanted to know how she could distinguish between a message from God and one from the devil, if she still believes the JFK assassination was a plot, and to ask her questions a skeptic might ask.

Brian:

Do you still believe that President Kennedy's assassination was a plot?

Jeane Dixon:

I believe it as sure as I'm sitting here. And remember that was not through telepathy. I had a revelation. It is not one person who did it and it will eventually be revealed. The truth is already known by some, but it has not been told.

Do you think you know who was involved?

Jeane Dixon:

Yes, I know the plot. Kay Halle will tell you that I went to her and said: "It's a plot," and I even got the name of the assassin. Now, this is very, very interesting. This power that comes from outer space. You see, the sun comes up in the morning and goes down at night. It goes round and round and round like this. Now, our lives go round and round and round like this, too. Now, when you're driving in a car and you have a radio on, and you go under a tunnel or a bridge, your reception stops, doesn't it? All right. Now, sometimes when I pick these things up, it will stop and I will only get the beginning and end of a word, not the middle [curiously, mediums in trance have a similar problem with names], or the end of a name and not the first part; or the first part of a name and sometimes not the end. That tells me that out here somewhere—in outer space—is a very powerful source of power for blockage. It could be some kind of gravitation. And that is when I got Oswald [assassin of JFK]. I got the first two letters and the last two and not the middle ones. And when I was on television with former ambassador to Moscow Joseph Davies [see chapter on Martha Rountree], I got the first and last letters of Khrushchev, but not the middle. So something very powerful out there is blocking that transmission, or channel, to me. That's one thing I'm working on, because I'd like to discover what it is. And I'm thinking about UFOs coming in the way there. That is the reason I'm doing an awful lot on UFOs. I haven't really touched on UFOs yet. I'm going to do a book on UFOs.

Is that your next book?

Jeane Dixon:
No, that's not my next book. I've got three next books. You know, the reason I am persecuted in so many places is because people think "she's all for President Nixon." The reason I am for President Nixon is that in 1949 I picked up the program of his life and said that one day he would be President of the United States and I have never changed that. And then in 1962, when Nixon said he was through with politics, I said he hasn't even begun his politics. Because I know the will of God, and we do not change that. And I know the difference in my vibrations.

This was not a revelation. I picked up the program of his life. That was the Holy Spirit.

Somewhere in your book you've got to show how the eternal flame in Arlington cemetery is going to bring about an eternal flame in us. I say that the knowledge of your faith is not enough; it's experience of your faith that truly counts. That is what I want to bring out in life. This is what I experienced. That is what Harry Morgan experienced.

The first book about Mrs. Dixon, A Gift of Prophecy, *by Ruth Montgomery, tells of a vision which Jeane Dixon had, that a baby born in the Middle East on February 5, 1962, would grow up to form a new Christianity and "bring together all mankind in one all-embracing faith." In a later book by Jeane Dixon,* My Life and

Prophecies, *this boy turns out to be the Anti-Christ. I asked Mrs. Dixon which version was accurate.*

Jeane Dixon:

It was not completely told in the first book. I was being told that this boy would be born in the Middle East and that he is going to turn out to be the Anti-Christ. People will follow him instead of the Lord. Remember, at first he is going to do an awful lot of good. Dear God, yes. And then the people are going to have the choice, their own free will, to go with him or the Lord. Now, Hitler at first was fantastically good for the poor, and Mussolini too, and they thought *they* were the power. If he kept on with what was good, instead of turning and thinking *he* was the power, this boy would be fantastically wonderful.

Will he be like Mussolini or Hitler?

Jeane Dixon:

He's going to be much more powerful, much greater. He will perform miracles. He's going to be absolutely a miracle worker. He has the eternal spirit in him that belongs to the Lord, and he is going to bring people to the very ecstacy of goodness, and he's going to lead them from despair. But, when he gets up there: "LOOK WHO I AM!" And then he's going to be powerful, and the people who follow him are the ones, as I said in my book, who will fall. To keep your faith, it's the long, hard road up. But it's the only road.

What sort of miracles will he perform?

Jeane Dixon:

He'll cure the sick. He will seem to imitate Christ's life on earth. He's eleven now and understands his satanic mission.

If, as you say, you can always tell the difference between a message from Satan and a message from God, doesn't this mean that Satan isn't very clever, in that he can't deceive you, a mere mortal?

Jeane Dixon:

Yes, he's very clever. Listen, he comes to my left, over here. He's just as clever and conniving as you can be. But there's some little thing that tells you "No!" And it's a different feel, a different vibration.

Now, this sounds crazy, but with the devil there's a feeling of green. I can't tell you how, but I have the feeling of green. Isn't that crazy?

But if you can tell it's the devil, through this vibration that's different, you, a mortal, can tell, and avoid him and his temptations; then he's not much of an adversary for God, is he?

Jeane Dixon:
Yes, he is. I'm going to tell you the way he is. He is so clever, that when he tempts you, you feel "maybe I'll try it. Maybe I'll take a chance." You see? "Maybe this time I can do it and get away with it." But you can't. And don't ever try it. It's sort of a feeling like this. There's a pull so strong that you have to pull the other way.

You make it sound like a magnet.

Jeane Dixon:
It is a magnet. It's an absolute magnet. It's a pull that's connected with your thoughts. Such as: "Do this to a person . . ." "They've done this to you; do this to them . . . Strike back. Strike back. Strike back."

Some people might call those normal human reactions to being hurt by somebody.

Jeane Dixon:
Yes. Strike back. But I will *not* strike back.

When you were conscious during your vision that the devil was coming to tempt you, was it anything specific he was trying to tempt you to do?

Jeane Dixon:
He was probably trying to tempt me to lose my faith. "It's tough. The road is hard. Let's take the easy road."

When you say the devil "is green" it sounds awfully pleasant, like grass and nature. And looking at green is supposed to cure headaches, you know?

Jeane Dixon (pointing up and over her left shoulder, as she stood in her room in the Breakers Hotel. Through the window behind her I could see the Atlantic waves batter the shore):

And he's always over here, to the left . . . I've seen him in green, and he's very bad-tempered, you know. And he pulls. And you have to pull physically, not only mentally. It's a physical pull, too.

You've seen him in green, in your dreams?

Jeane Dixon:

No, I haven't. Each time I've seen him in daylight. In plain daylight.

Why do you think he's manifesting himself to you?

Jeane Dixon:

He doesn't just manifest himself to me.

He might be here with us, now?

Jeane Dixon:

He's around us as much as the Lord is. And don't think he isn't. You bet your life. He's between us. And he's always pulling. And remember, physically he pulls, not only mentally.

I don't know what you mean.

Jeane Dixon:

Say I'm walking down to a drugstore and I have an allergy to chocolate soda and the doctor has told me: "You'll be sick if you take chocolate soda." But I want that chocolate soda so badly, there's a power that pulls me to it, and I have to use a stronger power to pull away . . . One time someone played a dirty trick on me. It was the most awful thing in the world. And there was the greatest pull for revenge. And it pulled me physically. Then I thought: "It's up to God, not me." He's the one to judge us, not me. And that's where our soul goes to on judgment day. So I placed my trouble in His hands and every day's a new day. I start the new day saying: "Please, Lord, help me to pull in this direction, not *this* direction."

Third Interview with Jeane Dixon: April 12, 1975

Jeane Dixon's husband, James, had been mugged and almost killed. Naturally I thought—why didn't she warn him? She had saved his life before when she persuaded him not to fly in a plane that subsequently crashed. Why, now, couldn't she have protected him from his nearly fatal injuries? That was the first of many questions I wanted to ask her. Here are my questions and her answers, a few days after the mugging.

Brian:

People will say how terrible that you couldn't foresee Jimmy being mugged.

Jeane Dixon:

But I did. I said: "Jimmy, don't go. Please don't go." And I waited at the door for him—that's the first time I waited at the door for him in twenty-eight years. Any other time I would have gone to bed.

He'll tell you that. And I had the telephone numbers of the doctors there and everything. It was that fast. And I kept a cool head because I just knew. And this is what Jimmy said as he went out the door. "They'll never get me." He meant that he would be as fast as they are—to protect himself. He's very strong, you see, physically. As he was going out the door, I said: "I'll wait here for you."

And you'd never waited at the door before?

Jeane Dixon:

Never.

Did you have a feeling that something would happen?

Jeane Dixon:

I sat there, and it's the funniest feeling in the world . . . You know when you drop something and you think it's going to hit your toe and you move your toe out of the way, that feeling between there . . . and there? When you drop the scissors or something? You get that same feeling. Or if you cut your finger or some scalding water falls on it? That's the feeling.

If you had meditated before Jimmy went out, do you think you would have known quite clearly that "if he goes out he's going to be attacked"?

Jeane Dixon:

If I had meditated on it, I would have seen it, yes. And when I say I would have seen it, I mean I would have known it would happen. We had company that evening. He went to see them to their car. It was cold, cold that evening. He was in his slacks and a sort of sports shirt; so he put on a very heavy coat and a fur hat he wears with it, the sort they wear in Russia, you know. I said: "Don't go!" He said: "Well, I want to see the people to the car." And I stood at the door and said: "Be careful."

Then, as he went out, our little dog, ferocious little dog, Teddy, went along with him. All Jimmy did was to walk across the street and about two steps up the sidewalk. And he said: "Teddy! Run!" So Teddy ran up to his little favorite green knoll that he has up there and claims as his own.

And then from nowhere comes this great big man, about 250 pounds. He said to Jimmy: "Give me your money." So Jimmy said: "I'll give you what I've got," and reached in his pocket and he had maybe a five-dollar bill and four one-dollar bills. The man said: "I want your wallet." Jimmy said: "I don't have a wallet." He didn't. The man said: "This isn't the kind of money I want." So he just hauled off and knocked Jimmy unconscious. That's all Jimmy remembers to begin with. That was on the outside sidewalk. Then there's those big, high cement flower boxes. We could tell by the blood where Jimmy was thrown over them, into the courtyard. Luckily he was unconscious so he didn't try to protect himself with his hands and arms—so when he fell they weren't broken.

But evidently they weren't satisfied with giving him a knockout blow. They tore his clothes to ribbons, cut the pockets out of his clothes—and you could see the dent in his hat where he fell: his hat saved him. Then they left him for dead.

You could tell Jimmy had tried to crawl—of course he was unconscious. He didn't know one thing from that first blow. But you can tell where he was thrown over from the outside walk, and you can tell where he crawled, from the trail of blood.

He wears glasses with steel frames around them and evidently the impact was so terrific from that knockout blow, that the lenses came out of the frames.

One was one place and another was the other place, but strangely enough the lenses weren't broken. And the dog chain was perhaps ten feet from where Jimmy was. I don't know how the dog chain got there. But the dog came home without him.

I was waiting at the door for Jimmy and I saw the dog coming and wondered what was the matter. And there was Jimmy staggering, trying to find his way home.

And he was just ripped and cut to pieces and trompled on and everything. He couldn't see. Blood was all over, coming out of his nose, his mouth, his ears. I thought: "Dear God!" But I was able —I had to keep my head—and I called Dr. Cahill. I said: "Jimmy's been hit, he's been hurt badly." I said: "Come immediately."

He was here in six minutes. He said: "Call an ambulance." I got the ambulance. From the time I made that first telephone call to the time Jimmy was in the emergency room was sixteen minutes—they even had the door open and the doctors waiting for him.

If it wasn't that everything was that fast, Jimmy wouldn't be here. Some of our friends who've gotten the same treatment didn't fare so well. Their knockout blows were knockouts for life.

[Shortly before I spoke to Mrs. Dixon about her husband, she made very specific predictions about Jacqueline Onassis and her family, and I wanted to know what extrasensory means she used.]

How long did you meditate before you made the predictions about Jacqueline Kennedy Onassis?

Jeane Dixon:

Oh, dear God, I meditated on that: it took my whole Easter Sunday and several other days and nights.

You say that there will be a conspiracy to defraud her out of her inheritance from Aristotle Onassis. Did you get that by telepathy?

Jeane Dixon:
That is telepathy, yes. I'm picking up thoughts.

How about your prediction that Caroline Kennedy's romances with older men will cause a split between her and her mother?

None of this, though, is through revelation?
That's precognition.

Then you say kidnapping threats will pose very real dangers to both Caroline and John, Jr. Do you get that by precognition?

Jeane Dixon:
No, no. That's telepathy.

So you're picking up the thoughts or conversation of the people who are planning the kidnapping?

Jeane Dixon:
Yes. They're thinking of it now. I can reach that far.

And when you predict that Jacqueline Onassis will experience loneliness until she eventually finds the right man in 1979—is that precognition on your part?

Jeane Dixon:
Yes.

None of this, though, is through revelation?

Jeane Dixon:
No, not revelation. It's not prophecy. It's not a vision. It's telepathy and precognition. You see, you don't change a vision. That's from a power greater than ours. These predictions about Jacqueline Onassis—they could be changed; but they're not going to be changed.

The Rockefeller Commission recently concluded that there is no evidence that the JFK assassination was other than what was found by the Warren Commission.

Jeane Dixon:
There was a definite plot that will eventually be revealed: I don't care what the Rockefeller Commission says.

The boy born in the East who will become the Anti-Christ; have you had any feelings about him lately?

Jeane Dixon:

No, I haven't meditated on him, though I think he's in Egypt at this time. He hasn't gone to Rome as yet.

You know you said that you knew Richard Nixon's life from birth to death. And you also said that he would come out of Watergate smelling like roses.

Jeane Dixon:

Historians yet unborn are going to take the facts and he's going to go down as a great President. They're going to find that the price the world is paying for trying to discredit Nixon is going to be that we'll practically lose our freedom.

FOURTH INTERVIEW WITH JEANE DIXON:
November 1975

To arrange for a final interview for this book, I called Mrs. Dixon at close to midnight on Saturday, November 22. She had just returned to her home after taking care of a sick neighbor.

Jeane Dixon:

I'm working like a dog. The lady next door is very, very sick and this is going on every night. She's eighty-four and she can't walk and has edema. . . . Now I want to help you, but could you call me at the office in the morning? I'm just dead, dead, dead. Call me and just keep on calling me till you get me, because we'll get your book finished. . . . I can hardly keep my eyes open. So I'd like to get a glass of milk and go to bed and then you call me . . . Good night.

November 23, 1975

Jeane Dixon:

I'm on another call here. Can you wait a moment? [When she returned to the phone she was crying.] I have to get over this upset condition. I'll tell you about it. The night before last I heard this awful crash about three in the morning. I ran into Jimmy's room and said: "Jimmy, how can you sleep through a crash like that?" So he came and he didn't see anything. But he got dressed and went out. He took the dog and went up and down the street and I watched from the window. I told him it sounded like a plane crash. But he couldn't see anything. And so we called my sister Evelyn [a pilot] and everything was all right with her. And, Denis, as God is my judge and I'm telling you the facts, I didn't sleep a wink that night. I was wider awake than I've ever been awake in my life. It was something like when I have a revelation—a prophecy. It was not an earthly state. And then I got up. I didn't eat any breakfast. And I was so wide awake. I had no lunch. I wanted nothing.

I came home at noontime because I knew I was going to have a busy day. This was Friday. I couldn't sleep. I lay down and took my rosary beads and I was saying my rosary as fast as I could—for the freedom of Hungary, for the freedom of the world, and I was sort of in a different world. I went back to the office but I couldn't keep my mind on my work. I slept a little bit last night [Saturday] and I woke up during the night and said to Jimmy: "There's a funeral. Someone's going to be killed in that crash." He said: "You're just dreaming." I said: "I'm not dreaming." And then I went off to sleep. Then, just as you called this morning I got another call. . . . And General Watts had been killed in his plane. Yesterday around five-thirty he was flying in [Oklahoma] and I understand the police on the highway saw his plane losing altitude and hit the top of the trees and crash and burn. . . . Now why couldn't I have been shown that? He would not have flown if I had told him. . . . I'll get over it and call you later. But we were very close friends. So why didn't the Lord show me it was his plane that was going to crash? [Throughout, Mrs. Dixon was obviously very upset.]

November 27, 1975
Thanksgiving Day

Brian:
The crash you heard. After it, did you only phone your sister Evelyn?

Jeane Dixon:
Yes, because my other brothers and sisters don't fly in planes. I knew it was a plane crash.

It's very difficult for me to talk about it at the moment. . . . I knew someone was killed, someone we loved. . . . I had this death, but I didn't know it was he. But I have told him several times: "General Watts, when you meet your Maker, it will be because you will have fallen asleep in your plane."

Did he ever tell you that he had fallen asleep in his plane?

Jeane Dixon:

No, but I don't see how he could have helped it. Because he works like I work.

Do you see General Watts as going to heaven now?

Jeane Dixon:

He has a guardian angel that is so great and so powerful I know he is going to the place where it is the best place to go.

In my 1972 interview with you, you didn't believe there was intelligent life on other planets. Recently you mentioned there was intelligent life on a sister planet to the earth on the far side of the sun.

Jeane Dixon:

At that particular time I hadn't gotten it. But since that time I've known of the sister planet.

Did you get it by meditation?

Jeane Dixon:

This is how most of the things come. You see, I release myself to see what I can pick up, and, before, I had limited myself to the moon and didn't try for any farther.

Since then I've given more time to meditation, more time to listening to what I feel, and the more time you give the more you get. This planet is exactly on the other side of the sun. And I think UFOs are associated with this sister planet. And I think we will land instruments on Jupiter and they'll give us a bird's-eye view.

Are there people like us on this planet?

Jeane Dixon:

I can't tell you, but I know there's life there. I can feel there's life there. And, Denis, when there's vibrations there's life. When there are no vibrations, then it's dead. I feel there is animal and plant life on this other planet, and that from it comes a rhythm of vibrations. And that means whatever is there is in tune with the universe.

22

Views of Two Catholic Priests

FATHER EUGENE B. GALLAGHER

A Jesuit priest who has made a special study of demoniac possession and exorcism, Father Eugene B. Gallagher, of Old St. Joseph's Church, Philadelphia, has been lecturing on such subjects for years. In fact, his talks about a real-life exorcism were the genesis for the novel *The Exorcist,* by William Blatty. Blatty was a student in one of Father Gallagher's classes. I interviewed him on March 8, 1974.

Brian:

Jeane Dixon speaks of the devil as a physical reality. A psychiatrist, Dr. Riesenman, discussing diabolic possession and exorcism, speaks about them as facts. Do you agree with them?

Father Gallagher:

Yes, physical in a sense that it is a thing; that the evil spirit is a personality really existing. He's not material but he's physical in the sense of an actually existing reality.

And the purpose is?

Father Gallagher:

It's an evil that God permits. I take this from Christ's own words and deeds in the New Testament. Apparently evil spirits are allowed to roam the earth until the end of the world and then they will be confined to the Abyss, as evil spirits near the lake of Galilee said to Christ, "So don't drive us out to the Abyss now, before the time. Send us into these 2,000 pigs instead." And Christ said: "Okay, go ahead." And they went down into the lake and drowned.

You think that in a way these "evil spirits" are enjoying themselves?

Father Gallagher:

Yes, they are. Because they hate God and they're irrevocably confirmed in evil. It's a kind of revengeful expression against God. They can't hate God, so they hate the next best thing; man made in the image and likeness of God.

The most feverish critics of Jeane Dixon say she's inspired by the devil.

Father Gallagher:

I don't think so, from what I've read of her.

You think if she were, her activities would be less friendly, less benign?

Father Gallagher:

That's correct. She's not anti-religion. I think she's a woman enjoying her intuitions and getting paid for it.

Do you have any strong views about Jeane Dixon as a prophet?

Father Gallagher:

I can only say what I've said in answer to a question about her in a couple of lectures: "She does a little better than Drew Pearson."

Do you believe God does reveal Himself to man in specific revelations, indicating what the future is going to be?

178 *Jeane Dixon: The Witnesses*

Father Gallagher:

Let's say this. God does reveal things in the Bible. He has told us very little about the future. He does tell us in the Bible, in the Old Testament, that there are two things no false god and no human person could know. He said: "I alone can predict the future actions of people. Go to your false gods and see if they can do that." And he says: "I alone know the innermost secrets of the heart." Only God knows your innermost thoughts insofar as your attitude toward that thought is concerned, whether you consent or dissent and so forth. In other words, the evil spirit would have to wait until you enter into an overt action to find out what you think about certain ideas he might have suggested to you.

So you think Jeane Dixon's ability is intuitive?

Father Gallagher:

I think she's a good huncher.

You don't think God is talking to her?

Father Gallagher:

No, I don't think so, at all. In fact I used to read her in the paper for laughs. I'm Sagittarius, and I have never found a line relevant to me. It would be morally wrong for anyone, including herself, to think that Jeane, of her own power, is predicting with certainty free future acts of her fellow citizens—only God can do that, and those who might have revelations from him. I hope Jeane Dixon had her readers, with no firm faith in her predictions, read her as I do occasionally, for amusement and entertainment. She's conducting a guessing game and a lot of people like to get in on the fun!

MONSIGNOR JAMES A. MAGNER,
PROCURATOR OF CATHOLIC UNIVERSITY OF AMERICA (retired)

Father Magner was quoted in *A Gift of Prophecy*, as follows: "Neither in idea nor expression is there any conflict between Mrs. Dixon's gift and the Church. In fact, to a Catholic it seems a rather normal thing, although we don't yet know very much about this field of psychic phenomena." That was in 1965. Ten years later, on June 3, 1975, I asked him:

Brian:

Do you think God communicates to individuals, as Jeane Dixon believes God communicates to her, through revelations?

Father Magner:

I certainly believe he communicates to individuals. I pray to God every day and I ask Him to help me, to instruct me, to enlighten me, to inspire me. In the same way I pray to the saints, because I believe in the communication of saints as they are in my present, and in the next life; and before the throne of God, that they have His ear, so to speak. And I pray to them likewise and ask them to intercede for me that I may have a better understanding of what I should do, give me the strength and courage to do what is right. And also, I pray for material things. I pray for health, and I may pray for success in this or that venture. I believe Christ Himself tells us to do that.

Is your approach to Mrs. Dixon entirely religious or do you have a scientific attitude as well?

Father Magner:

Partly both. I don't rule out the idea of direct spiritual or supernatural communication with God. But it's my thought that Mrs. Dixon may have some type of communication with the forces, electrical or otherwise, supersensory or extrasensory, about which we know very little.

Have you read extensively in the history of psychical research or parapsychology?

Father Magner:

No, I have not.

Do you have any doubts about Mrs. Dixon's abilities?

Father Magner:

I can't say that I have doubts. But one always says: "Well, I think I should know a little bit more about this before I pass a positive judgment."

When I spoke with her she talked of the devil as an absolute entity. Do you agree with her that the devil is an entity?

Father Magner:
  Yes.

Her severest critics suggest her gift is from the devil.

Father Magner:
  I wouldn't subscribe to that at all. Some of her writings, predictions, and so forth, I've found rather difficult to accept, but I've never found anything the slightest bit diabolical in them. I know Mrs. Dixon quite well personally and I find that she is a person who is very deeply religious, whose basic message really is the love of God. She goes to Mass every morning, I know she's a daily communicant, and she prays in church and asks for divine guidance. I cannot reconcile that with an allegation that she would be in communication with the devil.

I spoke to one priest who suggested Mrs. Dixon guesses and that she does "a little better than Drew Pearson."

Father Magner:
  Did any of them guess the assassination of President Kennedy?

That's a pretty well substantiated prediction of hers.

Father Magner:
  I think before statements of that kind were made, it might be well to tabulate the predictions which she has made and see which of them have been verified and which of them, let us say, have been paralleled by good guessers.

Do you have any general feeling about ESP?

Father Magner:
  I don't know, first of all, what the source of communication is when we speak of ESP. It may be a revelation from God, or a communication from God in one form or another, or it may be in some instances types of material radiation. I think we're just on the threshold of understanding the meaning of intelligence and the activity of the brain and I believe that as time goes on we may

find that there are forms of electrical communication which don't, necessarily, deal with the future, but which deal with thoughts and intentions of minds outside our own.

What do you think of Mrs. Dixon's astrology column?

Father Magner:
She told me that as a young girl she came into communication with a Jesuit priest and he gave her some ideas along these lines.

Of course, a Jesuit priest could be quite an eccentric man.

Father Magner:
Well, he could. As a matter of fact I asked Mrs. Dixon if her astrology columns—which by the way are carried all over the world—serve a useful purpose. And she said, yes, that she tried to give inspiration; or useful, or cheerful or optimistic ideas. And I said: "Couldn't I run one?" She said: "I think you could." So that may carry some of its own explanation. But I would say from my personal contacts with Mrs. Dixon, there's no question, she is a good person, and she preaches, she really preaches at me, too, and she does most of the talking in the times when we meet. And her discussion is about the love of God and the importance of good religion.

How do you like her preaching to you?

Father Magner:
It's all right. I think maybe I need it now and then.

23

Jeane Dixon: For and Against

Although I set out to interview witnesses for or against Jeane Dixon, and proposed to let the reader be the judge, I realize that because of my part in the investigation I, too, have become a witness.

My opinion is evident in this second and final interview with Daniel St. Albin Greene of *The National Observer* on January 4, 1974—and so is his.

Brian:

I'd like to make two brief observations. One is that although I think your evidence in your National Observer *article about Jeane Dixon is remarkably persuasive, I still think it's a mystery.*

Greene:

Oh yes. I'm the first to admit that some parts of the Jeane Dixon story are still a mystery. She keeps it that way.

Brian:

The other point is this: I don't think you've been fair as a newspaperman, as an objective reporter, to Jeane Dixon's psychic ability. She has made some remarkably accurate predictions to intelligent people, who back each other up in confirming those predictions. You skipped over them in your article.

Greene:

The article was trimmed a bit at the end because it ran so long. I had devoted at least half the article to an assessment of Jeane Dixon the psychic. If it had run any longer, I would have provided more evidence to back up my premise that Jeane Dixon is not a prophet. I investigated a number of her famous predictions. I tried to find people who would corroborate them. I've talked to several people who were supposed to know something about the Bobby Kennedy prediction. It just does not hold up. The John F. Kennedy prediction—I did talk to a few people who did say: "Yes, she said that to me." But I've talked to people since then who have known her very well for years, who claim they can prove she never made that prediction.

Brian:

You didn't speak with Ira Walsh, a Hearst executive on the West Coast?

Greene:

No, I did not talk to Ira Walsh.

Brian:

And he's backed up by a TV executive, Tom Swafford, whom you didn't get to either, I imagine.

Greene:

No I don't know the name. I'm not a complete disbeliever. I believe there may be something called ESP, but I can't explain it. You have to show me pretty firm evidence, which I've never been shown.

One thing that makes me suspicious of prophets is that they all use the same system. They're always predicting calamities. They're always predicting sicknesses or assassinations or global problems. And if they predict enough of these, some are bound to come true. A person like Jeane Dixon is constantly telling people that something dire is going to happen. Now, most of these things do not happen. But occasionally they do, and then her believers swear to God that Jeane Dixon prophesied it.

Brian:

This is what I think. I think she's got something. For the

*sake of argument, I think she makes ten genuine predictions in a
year that come true, often about people close to her. But then she
clouds these with dozens of predictions about celebrities and national and international events for which she's using her intuition
or merely making intelligent guesses, and only a small proportion
of these come true.*

Greene:

I have talked to a number of people who first joined Jeane because they believed she was a holy woman, and wanted to be a
part of her life. But these people sooner or later learned the truth,
and now they say: "She's just not what I thought she was."
They're disillusioned.

Brian:

*With the genuine predictions, what seems to happen is that
when it comes closer to the date of the predicted event, she becomes more specific and more emotional.*

Greene:

If she really does have *something*, as you suggest, I think some
way should have been found in all these years for her power to
have been absolutely proven. You know as well as I do that she's
declined time after time to be tested by any reputable scientist.

Brian:

*I think she's got something. For example, when she says to a
friend [Martha Rountree]: "Don't go into that house, I beg
you!" And soon after the house burns to the ground.*

Greene:

My uncle used to do the same thing. My uncle swears—and
he's been nothing but a house painter all his life—that on two or
three occasions when relatives died, he saw visions of the death before it happened. Now, that doesn't make him a prophet. I don't
know what it makes him. It may mean he's an overly sensitive
person or a person with an extraordinary amount of tragic intuition—I don't know. It may just be nonsense that he talks when
he's drinking or something. You know, thousands of people have
premonitions. Have you heard of the Premonitions Bureau?

Brian:
Sure I have.

Greene:
They've got I don't know how many reports of premonitions, that either came true or didn't. But the people who made these do not go around and make a lot of money calling themselves prophets.

Brian:
I think there's truth in both our points of view. I don't think that either one of us is absolutely right.

Greene:
[Laughs.] A few years ago I finally reached the point of educational accomplishment when I discovered that I'll never know everything, and that many things I have learned are wrong, and that there's nothing wrong with changing one's mind. I started calling myself an intelligent man when I reached that point.

24

Jeane Dixon's Vision

While meditating in St. Matthew's Cathedral in October 1974, Jeane Dixon saw a pair of red boots march across the altar in a determined manner.

Her first thought was: "The devil wears red boots."

She looked again at the altar and now she saw the twelve apostles.

In an effort to understand these visions, she fasted and prayed for three days. Then, at two in the morning, she awoke to a dazzling display of lights and colors over her bed.

She sensed that the lights were a symbol of God, that the red boots had been a symbol of Evil, and that the message was that in the coming battle between Good and Evil, Good would triumph.

During the next two weeks she had a series of vivid, detailed visions that left her emotionally drained, but exhilarated. "I saw pictures and heard voices in my mind," explains Mrs. Dixon. "Perhaps, like a child who hears grown-ups talking, I only understood part of the conversation. Perhaps I glimpsed it all. I don't know."

She recalls seeing two men setting up electric wiring in a research laboratory and they appeared to be monitoring the dreams of people sleeping in two adjoining rooms.

Jeane Dixon watched them in her trancelike vision and saw the sleepers change size, race, and several times change sex.

She took this to mean that God had chosen to give these people such bodies in different lives and that she was witnessing a speeded-up version of their reincarnations.

She "saw" a surgeon in a hospital laboratory whose brain seemed gigantic and crammed with knowledge from his previous lives. And he took the accumulated knowledge with him to the operating table. Mrs. Dixon sensed after this vision that secrets which died with scientists of the past will be revived and diseases will be defeated; medical techniques and theories conceived long ago but never practiced because they were thought heretical or way-out, will be tried and prove effective.

Jeane Dixon's visions of reincarnation echo her own intuition: she feels she lived before in a mountainous region where the air was cold and thin and her companions were monks. In fact, she believes she may have been, in a previous life, a holy man in a Tibetan monastery.

But her three nights of visions that stretched into November, were not all of reincarnation. She saw Copernicus and then a giant radio telescope and this recalled her previous prediction that we would contact another civilization before the end of this century.

She was left with the conviction that before the end of the twentieth century, ordinary people will be able to use telepathy and it will be considered a natural way for friends to communicate with one another. And the sick, she believes, will use faith healing to cure themselves.

It is rare for Mrs. Dixon to have visions of such a positive and hopeful nature, but she pointed out that what she "saw and heard" is not going to happen tomorrow. "At first some people will use the knowledge of their past lives for evil," she said. "That is what the devil's boots meant in my first vision. But Good will eventually triumph. Then wars and personal hatreds will end and man will share his knowledge with the rest of the world."

In a talk, a few weeks later (November 26, 1974), Mrs. Dixon told members of the Northern Palm Beach County Board of Realtors: "In Washington, D.C., my hometown, real estate offices are starting to close down. The listings are there, the realtors are there, the buyers are there—but the money isn't there." But she consoled them with her belief that Florida realtors would do better than those in any other state during the recession.

"The economy will not get any better for the time being," she went on.

"God gave us Nixon to divide us . . . to test us where our faith is concerned, to see if we could come together."

In answers to questions by reporters, Jeane Dixon said: "Future historians will uncover startling revelations about the Watergate scandal. We have only seen the tip of the iceberg. Within a year and a half, the American people will learn of cover-ups regarding Pearl Harbor, the Bay of Pigs, Vietnam, and the Warren Commission's report on the assassination of John Kennedy."

"In 1976, two doctors will get the American Medical Association to accept a cure for cancer—a cure that is in existence now."

"In 1978, you will see a different Spiro Agnew back on his way up again. He will explain many things in a new book."

"We're going to have one of the biggest civil wars you ever could imagine. An organization of geniuses has outlined it already. This conflict will begin in 1978."

"By the end of the 1970s, not only sources of fuel and energy, but also transportation and communication companies will be under government control. The last to be nationalized will be the steel industry."

"The world will not end for another 3,000 to 5,000 years, when the sun and earth will collide."

As she walked through the lobby of Palm Beach's Breakers Hotel, where she gave her talk to the realtors, Jeane Dixon was stopped by a gray-haired man.

"Are you really a prophetess?" he asked.

"I'm just plain Jeane Dixon," she replied with a smile. "A plain human being. A plain citizen." And then she let him know her philosophy. "I want to help others to help themselves. God has given me a talent to do that."

She touched his fingertips lightly and said: "When you get older your heart is not going to be as strong as it is today. Take care of yourself—it's important."

A cartoon published soon after, in a local paper, was captioned

"God gave us Nixon to divide us.—Jeane Dixon." And the cartoon showed a cloud with a voice coming out of it, saying: "Don't blame me. I voted for McGovern."

If I know Jeane Dixon, she would have laughed, too.

THE MESSIAH
OR
CHRIST'S SECOND COMING

At a meeting sponsored by the Lakeport Women's Club in Laconia, New Hampshire, on October 21, 1975, Mrs. Dixon predicted:

"The greatest work of Alexander Solzhenitsyn is yet to come. It will be a work of the spirit which will spark new fire in the hearts of cynics all over the world. He will become the center of an international movement to restore religious faith to the world, including his own Russia, which will be converted.

"Scientists will discover still living creatures long thought to be extinct.

"The entire Middle East is on the brink of a glorious new era and will be to the modern world what the Italian Renaissance was to the sixteenth century."

At the end of the century, she said, Canada and Brazil will be among the most powerful countries because they'll have both food and energy.

She predicted that in this century, we'll be able to land equipment on Jupiter and expressed her belief that life exists on a sister planet to the earth, on the far side of the sun.

"There are many here tonight," said Mrs. Dixon to her audience of more than seven hundred, "who will experience what will happen in Jerusalem." She said that the Jews would feel it is the coming of their Messiah, and Christians, that it is the second coming of Christ.

No one knows exactly when it will happen, she said, reminding her audience that the Bible says not even the angels in heaven know it.

"We will all witness the shadow of the cross, the tremor of the earth, and three days of darkness."

25

John Nebel, JFK, and Lee Harvey Oswald

As the deadline for this book to reach my publisher grew nearer, I was eager to track down as much evidence as possible in the few days left. Was there some witness who would clinch it: give conclusive evidence that Jeane Dixon made a prediction that was right on target, and could not be explained away? Or would there be a witness who could demolish the whole phenomenon as fantasy, or a skillful confidence trick played by a persuasive woman on the innocent?

And then I found my witness.

He was John Nebel, who hosts a radio talk show from midnight to six in the morning on WMCA in New York City.

Reputedly, 100,000 listeners jam the lines every fifteen minutes trying to speak with Nebel. Fortunately, I phoned him at a quarter to midnight, on June 19, 1975, before the show went on the air.

This is what he said:

Nebel:
Jeane Dixon was on my show on January 23, 1963. Someone

asked Mrs. Dixon: "Who do you think President Kennedy's Republican opponent will be in next year's election?"

Mrs. Dixon said, in a very sad voice, that not only would Kennedy not run in '64, but that he would be killed by an assassin before the end of 1963.

I quickly switched to a commercial and while we were off the air I told everyone not to refer to Mrs. Dixon's prediction when we went on the air again. And Mrs. Dixon said she understood my concern.

Now, by an extraordinary coincidence, the very next night, about an hour before air time, Lee Harvey Oswald phoned me. He wanted to get on the show. He said he had a fare to come in from Louisiana and he wanted to be on to talk about fair play for Cuba—not the organization itself—but he was talking about the philosophy of being fair. And, then, in order to give me some other goodies, he had defected to Russia and married a girl there and came back, and so forth and so on. But I just didn't dig it. So the outcome of it was I said no. And then he turned around; he called me a son-of-a-bitch, a fag, and what have you.

Brian:

He was calling you long distance?

Nebel:

Yes, and he paid for the call.

So, from Louisiana he couldn't possibly have heard your show the previous night when Jeane Dixon predicted JFK's assassination?

Nebel:

No, he couldn't possibly have heard it. Oswald indicated to me that he had been a listener of mine when he was living in Greenwich Village and he gave me a lot of bullshit about how great I was and knowledgeable and all that sort of crap that went with it. I had no interest at all. I had never heard of Oswald in my life. I just scribbled his name on a slip of paper and put it in a file—which I looked up after the assassination.

Another thing that happened with Jeane Dixon. On the Sunday prior to the assassination she called me on the phone. And she told me she was on her way to brunch with the widow of a man who had been concert master for the United States Marine Band. And Mrs. Dixon said, as she was passing the White House she saw a shroud over it. She said to me on the phone: "Something is going to happen to Jack this week." She called him Jack.

Well, I must admit to you I did not get excited about that. I'm certainly not going to use that on the air. So I thanked her very much and said that I was delighted she had called and all; but it was meaningless to me—because if he got hit by a car she would claim that was her prediction. And I knew damn well nothing was going to happen to him.

So now it's Friday, the day of the assassination.

Maybe around eleven-thirty, a quarter of twelve, maybe it had already hit noontime, she called me and said she'd had brunch with the same lady, the concert master's widow, and she was so concerned when she went by the White House because there was a shroud over it, even darker than the prior Sunday. She said that she knew, I think it was a relative of Jack's, and she had contacted him and told him not to go into the parade, not to be involved in any political thing in Dallas today—that something's going to happen.

Well, I accepted that the same way as I did the prior Sunday story. I wasn't interested. I didn't tell her that. I thanked her very much.

About quarter after one I received a call from a fellow who said: "Turn on your TV!" And he hung up. Because he was anxious to get back to his. I found out who he was later—didn't recognize his voice at the time.

So I turned on my TV and any place you turned the dial you would hit the story.

Now, I'm sort of a non-believer—and yet that's pretty exciting.

Some people have implied that Jeane Dixon's prediction about JFK's assassination was a self-fulfilling prophecy, in that Oswald might have heard of her prediction and decided to make it a reality. But you're convinced, are you, that he never heard the radio show on which she made the prediction—although he phoned you the next night?

Nebel:

I'm absolutely convinced he never heard that show. But I don't believe Oswald was the assassin. I think it was a conspiracy.

So, though you're a non-believer, Mr. Nebel, do you think her prediction about Kennedy was remarkable?

Nebel:

Well, I'd have to say that—if she'd given me Robert Kennedy and a couple of others.

That would have made you a believer?

Nebel:

It would have given me greater interest in the possibility. Of course she'd bombed a lot of times, too, you know.

Yes, but all psychics do.

Nebel:

I agree.

I hope you eventually read this book. I think you'll find her powers more persuasive.

Nebel:

Sir, I've got to get on the air.

Have a good show.

Nebel:

Thank you . . . [It was almost ten after midnight.]

[John Nebel is still a non-believer—yet he testified that Jeane Dixon told him three times that President Kennedy would be assassinated—the last time from three quarters to half an hour before it happened.]

ANOTHER WITNESS

But I still wanted another witness to confirm that Jeane Dixon had predicted over the air that JFK would be assassinated. Presumably hundreds of thousands of New Yorkers had heard the broadcast—but that was twelve years ago and would any of them have cause to recall the exact details?

John Nebel said that Jacqueline Susann was a guest on the show. But she had died on September 21, 1974.

Hoping that Jacqueline Susann might at least have mentioned Jeane Dixon to her husband, movie producer Irving Mansfield, I traced him to the Beverly Hills Hotel and asked.

This was what Irving Mansfield said, on June 25, 1975:

John Nebel's absolutely right. After Jeane Dixon predicted John Kennedy would be assassinated, Nebel switched straight to a commercial. I was there in the studio, but not on the show. During the commercial Nebel said: "Let's not discuss the assassination prediction."

Nebel said that broadcast was January 23, 1963. But it was much closer to the date of the assassination than that. I tell you why I know. Jackie was doing interviews to promote her first book, *Every Night, Josephine!* She had already done some TV shows, but they're recorded two or three weeks in advance of being shown. Nebel's was a live radio show, and the first one Jacqueline Susann did—about two days before the book's publication date. We gave Long John an exclusive in a sense—her first live radio show. And that was in November 1963.

I believe President Kennedy was assassinated one day after the book's publication.

So in fact, Jeane Dixon made the prediction only a few days before it happened.

[I checked back with John Nebel and he explained the discrepancy in dates by saying Jeane Dixon was on his show several times in 1963 and made the JFK assassination prediction more than once.]

President Franklin Roosevelt

Finally, with time running out, I tried to get confirmation that Jeane Dixon had been called to the White House by President Franklin Roosevelt.

Jeane Dixon says she went at least twice: on a Thursday in November 1944, and in mid January 1945, a few months before his death.

Her critics say there is no official evidence to confirm those visits.

What is the official evidence?

The National Archives and Records Service in Washington, D.C., don't have any information about the visits.

The Secret Service says its policy prohibits commenting on the President's or former Presidents' appointments or itinerary.

The Franklin D. Roosevelt Library can neither affirm nor deny that Jeane Dixon visited Franklin Roosevelt. "Her name does not appear in the White House appointment diaries for the periods involved, and we are unable to find elsewhere in the papers here any evidence that she met with the President. However, Mr. Roosevelt was in Washington at the times mentioned so we cannot say it was impossible for them to have met."

Jim Bishop offers no clues for or against the visits in his book *FDR's Last Year.* But he does record the mysterious behavior of FDR's doctor, Vice-Admiral McIntire, who, on November 18, 1944 (about the time Mrs. Dixon claims she first visited FDR), wrote to a fellow doctor: "The President is in excellent health." He wrote this even though Commander Bruenn, a heart specialist, had informed McIntire that FDR had irreversible hypertensive heart disease, was losing weight, and had high blood pressure. "As a physician," writes Jim Bishop, "McIntire understood the situation but denied it. His daily reports from Bruenn became Navy secrets."

Bishop's detailed book reveals that FDR never once asked his physicians even the most casual questions about his own state of health.

Yet Roosevelt is known to have been a man of insatiable curiosity.

Could Dr. Bruenn solve the mystery? I asked him, on November 11, 1975.

He said: "By November 1944 [the date of Mrs. Dixon's first reported visit] I had been taking care of President Roosevelt for eight months. There is no question that he was a sick man, but it certainly did not impair his mental faculties. When the chips were down, he was right there.

"As far as I can recall Bishop's book, he thought the President was mentally incapable of carrying on his work. This was distinctly not so. I was in fairly intimate contact with him practically every day for the last year or more, and there's no question in my mind that he was functioning well.

"I understand Elliott Roosevelt believes his father may have kept silent because 'what you don't know can't hurt you.' My interpretation of why the President never asked questions about his health is that he felt himself to be a man of destiny—in the sense that he had a job to do and there was nothing going to stop him— neither his health nor his political opponents."

But surely a sick man determined to finish a job wants to know if he has a chance of surviving long enough to do it?

Whatever his motives, it is clear that President Roosevelt didn't ask his doctors: "How much longer do I have?" or even: "What's wrong with me?" and that they didn't volunteer the information. In fact, Dr. Bruenn couldn't have answered the first question. "The President's death," he says, "was quite unexpected."

In this atmosphere, FDR sending for a psychic who was enthusiastically talked about in diplomatic circles begins to sound plausible.

I asked Jeane Dixon if she could explain why her name was not recorded in the White House visitors' book.

Did FDR ask you to keep the visits secret?

Jeane Dixon:
Never. Nobody asked me.

Why did you keep them secret? (Until twenty years after his death.)

Jeane Dixon:
If you asked me a question privately, I am not going to discuss it with someone else. I believe a confidence is a confidence. How in the world could I build up a reputation if I talked? I abhor gossip and I don't like anyone to betray a confidence.

Are there quite a few people, to your knowledge, who visit U. S. Presidents privately and aren't listed in appointments books?

Jeane Dixon:
Yes, there are. But when I visited President Roosevelt it was

mutually understood that my visit would not be recorded. I wanted it that way, so that doors wouldn't be closed to me; and FDR was able to call me and others can call me today without fear of publicity. I recall when I first met President Roosevelt, his valet asked me if I wanted tea or coffee, and when I said "Neither," he left us alone together. The President had a beautiful spiritual mind and he had great vision. He didn't ask me how much longer he had to live. He wanted to know: "How much more time do I have to do my work?"

FINAL WITNESSES: FDR's DAUGHTER AND SON

Her critics, I knew, would not accept Jeane Dixon's word alone as proof of her FDR visits. His daughter, Anna, who lived with her father for the last year of his life and in whom FDR confided, surely had heard something of the visits.

I called her and asked. But Anna was as unhelpful as the official documents. She knew nothing of any Jeane Dixon visits to her father.

Anna Roosevelt Halsted seemed to be the final deadend, as far as getting irrefutable evidence. If she didn't know, who would?

Once again, radio talk show host John Nebel gave me a lead. Speak to Betty Beale of the Washington *Star*, he suggested.

Betty Beale recalled a conversation with FDR's son Elliott, in which Jeane Dixon's White House visits were discussed.

I reached Elliott Roosevelt in England, where he now lives, on September 16, 1975.

He said:

I know Jeane Dixon quite well. She predicted two things for me and both came true. She predicted to my wife, just prior to the election, that I would be defeated for re-election to the mayoralty of Miami Beach. It wasn't likely that I'd lose. But she was right: I did lose. And she predicted, to my wife again, that I'd have difficult times ahead as regards my health. That has come true, too.

Jeane Dixon had access to the White House and I think she had a number of invitations. I remember father speaking of her on a couple of occasions and I think he talked about the fact of her prognostications. On several different occasions my father and I discussed the ability to project thoughts and other aspects of ESP. The subject interested him.

Yes, my father knew Jeane Dixon. And he did mention she had been to the White House on occasion. He knew her.

26

Summing Up

Some think the universe was created by a superman with a penchant for hymn singing and need for constant reassurance that He's the greatest. Some think everything is an accident. Others regard the universe and its creator, if any, as an outsize mystery and themselves as detectives.

I side with the detectives, and that is also my attitude to extrasensory perception. The evidence for ESP is good and growing— and the evidence that Jeane Dixon is capable of clairvoyance and precognition is persuasive. But is there an alternative explanation? Let's see.

The Witnesses

During the thirteen years Sir Walter Raleigh was imprisoned in the Tower of London under death sentence, he took his mind off the ax by doing chemical experiments and writing. He completed one volume of a multi-volume history of the world. Then, the story goes, a violent fight took place outside his cell. He and several others saw the whole thing. When called to give evidence about the fight, he found that he and all the other witnesses, without exception, had seen different fights. Disillusioned in the possibility of writing an objective history of anything—he dropped the project.

Aware of this weakness, I was surprised that the witnesses I questioned were unusually consistent in their testimony. I gave them the chance to exaggerate: they didn't take it. I put words in their mouths: they took them out. I interviewed some several times, approaching the questions I wanted answered from different angles: the answers never varied in substance. Now, they were not repeating a well-rehearsed fantasy, because in every instant their recollections coincided with known facts.

Even Father Cleary, suffering from a $3-million disappointment, said: "I do know of several instances where she dealt with other people and she was right on target. . . . I don't see any spirituality in it. Anyone who claims they have a direct line to God is deluded."

And her first biographer, Ruth Montgomery, disillusioned with Mrs. Dixon for personal reasons, told me: "There's no question that I believed Jeane had special powers or I never would have written the book. I think she had the gift then."

But is Jeane Dixon's gift not extrasensory, but perhaps an acutely developed sensory awareness? Did she predict the death of Justice Frank Murphy because she saw the man—and he looked deathly ill? I tried to fill the gap in my investigation, and answer the question by discussing that point with the woman the judge had planned to marry, Joan Cuddihy.

She said, on August 18, 1975:

I truthfully don't believe in psychics. I have a skepticism about anything like that. But I don't think Jeane Dixon would have known he was going to die—if she did—just by looking at him. He was in very, very good shape, I would say. I spoke to him a great many times. I had letters from him all during that period and he never complained of any illness. He was probably tired at the end, but all the Supreme Court Justices are tired at the end of court term. But for a man of fifty-six he was in very good health and he was kind of a health addict. He never drank, not even coffee. He'd only drink tea. And he didn't smoke.

He went home to Michigan because it was vacation time and he was having his annual checkup as he did for many years. There was no suspicion that he was ill when he went in. I spoke to him the night before he died. He called me from a public telephone, probably in a hall in the hospital. We had a very pleasant conversation, talking about my going out there.

And the next day I heard on the radio that he had died. I don't think they ever really discovered the cause of his death: his heart just stopped.

But his tests were good. I have a letter from the doctor who was head of Henry Ford Hospital, saying that Justice Murphy had passed all tests.

Brian:

So would you say that, if in fact Jeane Dixon had said to Eleanor: "Justice Murphy is not going to get married, you are going to have a new job, and someone close to you, but not a relative, is going to die"—that it appears to point to what in fact did happen?

Cuddihy:

Yes.

And, from what you say, Mrs. Dixon would have no normal way of coming to that conclusion?

Cuddihy:

That's right. But, even so, I don't believe Mrs. Dixon has ESP.

[That seems to eliminate the likelihood of Jeane Dixon picking up fairly obvious physical clues to the Justice's imminent death. Although I did learn from Frank J. Sladen, physician-in-chief at Henry Ford Hospital, that Justice Murphy "had some symptoms from his heart ever since a nasal operation."]

SKEPTICS AND BELIEVERS

Skeptics and the disillusioned dismiss her as a woman who made a few lucky guesses and parlayed them through a best-selling book and coast-to-coast TV and radio appearances into a worldwide reputation for prophecy.

Hardline skeptics say she's an impossibility, by denying that ESP exists despite a century of painstaking research that clearly indicates it does; so they label her as deluded or a master fake.

Does she, in fact, get some of her "psychic" information from more down-to-earth sources? I believe she does.

Mrs. Dixon once told me that she was able to keep a secret. One of those, I feel sure, is the identity of many of the famous and powerful who come to her for help, advice, and to forecast their futures. Some politicians may consider it a shortcut to God, or the twentieth-century way of prayer. But from them, it seems likely, Mrs. Dixon must get, perhaps entirely unconsciously, inside information that would help her in some predictions.

Staunch believers will have none of this. To them, every word she utters—almost—has a divine source.

And of course there are those on the middle ground: skeptics who say she may have something and believers who acknowledge she's not flawless.

ARE PSYCHICS REAL?

According to scientists throughout the world who should know, parapsychologists—enough experiments have been done to indicate that clairvoyance and precognition are facts of life. They're not sure about telepathy, which could be masquerading as clairvoyance and vice versa.

Aside from controlled experiments in laboratories, Dr. Louisa Rhine has studied over 15,000 cases of spontaneous ESP revealed to her over the years by people who claim they dreamed of an event before it happened, or were aware of a current happening through something other than their five senses. And to dismiss all of these reports, quite often verified by several witnesses, as coincidences, manifestations of insanity, fabrications, or faulty reporting, is unreasonable, or a knee-jerk reaction of those with no room for the unknown in their lives.

No question that the world of psychics is overpopulated with fakes. Literature on the subject of those caught in the act outnumbers accounts of those never caught, roughly fifty to one. But diamonds do exist among the dirt. There are several of spotless reputation, who survived every test scientists could bring to bear —one was even investigated by detectives and found completely honest. These psychics produced remarkable evidence of having the ability to obtain information by extrasensory means. Among them are Leonora Piper, Gladys Osborne Leonard, Estelle Roberts, Mrs. A. W. Verrall, Mrs. Willett, Mrs. Holland (a sister of Rudyard Kipling), and more recently, Eileen Garrett and Ena Twigg—all women, incidentally.

THE REAL WORLD?

These days the cause-and-effect world is shrinking and the alternative frustrates those scientists who want everything explained through mechanics or electromagnetism. And seeping into the picture comes the extrasensory world with all that implies.

The world Jeane Dixon inhabits has dimensions which we non-psychics or latent psychics visit only in our dreams and perhaps when half asleep, if at all. While wide awake we watch President Kennedy's flag-draped coffin and the riderless horse—Jeane Dixon, also wide awake, sees Kennedy dancing on his coffin. Is hers or ours the reality—or are they both fact, but she is seeing what is hidden from us?

Christ reportedly appeared to disciples three days after his death and not as an apparition. Perhaps these men were psychics, too. But, way out as it seems, Jeane Dixon's experience of seeing Kennedy jigging on his own coffin is echoed by other psychics.

Eileen Garrett tells of seeing her uncle after his death, as though he were still alive. Ena Twigg went to the funeral service for Britain's Air Chief Marshal Lord Dowding in Westminster Abbey and writes in her book *Ena Twigg: Medium:* "Lord Dowding appeared between two vases of roses at the altar; at full attention, saluting. He was radiant and looked thirty years younger—as he must have looked during the Battle of Britain."

Mrs. Twigg says: "When I am clairvoyant, I see spirit forms both mentally and objectively . . . Before a spirit form actually appears, I see a piercing bright light, and then the form builds up under the light."

Jeane Dixon says: "I really believe there are spirits around us."

REVELATION?

Before God communicates with her, she says, there are three days when the world is illumined with an unearthly light and she senses that she is to be given a revelation. Here she seems to share a world with mystics—a world others believe they can reach through drugs, fasting, or by mortifying the flesh.

Not being able to interview God, I can't say if Jeane Dixon is one of His prophets. The prophets of Old Testament days were said to have come to an end after the fall of the Temple and the gift was given to fools and children. This may be an analogy of the facts, in that, perhaps, true prophets retain their childlike innocence and faith, and that the sophisticated would stifle the gift, or let it atrophy, as an embarrassment. Not being able to read Mrs. Dixon's mind, it is impossible to refute her claims.

FAR REACHES OF THE MIND

Despite the magnificent explorers of the mind and brain, despite Freud and William James and Wilder Penfield, despite the scientists in their dream labs and others experimenting with hypnosis—the mind is still an enormous mystery.

But researchers do believe the following to be true: Under hypnosis, in dreams, in the sleepy state between sleep and awake, or during meditation, a person is more likely to experience what is called the extrasensory—a true glimpse of future events, or a current event occurring elsewhere, or the answer to a problem previously unsolved. This is when the mind is most relaxed and perhaps when part of it shifts into another gear—from neutral to supernatural!

Scientists in the Western world and Russia agree that the power of a psychic can't be pinned down. It comes and goes with as little warning as a hiccough or a firefly's glow. It can rarely be called up at will. Many pretend to have psychic power but few can successfully demonstrate it under test conditions. It cannot yet move mountains, though it can move objects the size of moles.

For Jeane Dixon, who claims to have telepathy, clairvoyance, and precognition, these fleeting feelings may happen any time—at lunch, in the bath, walking in the street. But are the messages she gets extrasensory?

Dr. Louisa Rhine, probably more familiar with spontaneous cases of ESP than anyone, says: "The criterion for judging whether an experience involves ESP is simple. It must be one that brings information new to the person and that brings it without mediation."

I decided not to address myself to Jeane Dixon's predictions of cosmic catastrophes in the distant future. It would be like shadowboxing. At best you miss, at worst you bruise your fist on a wall. And I have no interest in following up her twice-yearly predictions about the destiny of nations and marriages of movie stars.

It is her spontaneous, often emotional, always spur-of-the-moment expressions of ESP which intrigue me and which I find most convincing and most subject to investigation.

Which do I find most convincing? Incidents involving Frank Sinatra, Jr., John Kennedy, Robert Kennedy, the astronauts. I would include the blaze that destroyed Martha Rountree's home, the murder of Kitty Von Ammon's daughter, the death of Justice Frank Murphy, and, closer to home, Jeane Dixon's warning to her husband not to fly in a plane which in fact did crash on the flight he had planned to take.

Perhaps most impressive of all these is her prediction that the three astronauts would die by fire, during the plugs-out-test, and her pinpointing the cause of the fatal fire, after the event, but before the official investigation which confirmed her prediction.

HEALING THE SICK

No one has grown another limb after a visit to Lourdes or restored a severed artery to its former state by attending a faith-healing service. But when an illness is caused or sustained by the mind, then the mind seems capable of a cure, too.

This, I believe, Mrs. Dixon was able to do—helping James Harkins lose his warts overnight and also the pain in his legs. I spoke with others who think Mrs. Dixon helped cure their illnesses. And doctors confirmed that they had been cured.

Is there scientific evidence of such healing? Dr. Bernard Grad, a
Montreal biologist, experimented with Colonel Oskar Estebany
and published the results in the *Journal of the American Society
for Psychical Research*, volume 50, in 1965. He said that Estebany
could effect the accelerated healing of wounded mice by holding
his hands over them. In tests conducted by Dr. Justa Smith of Rosary Hill College, Buffalo, New York, in 1967, Estebany and three
other healers held their hands over flasks containing enzymes. All
four of them were able to speed up or slow down the activity of
the enzymes in such a way that it would have effected body
healing. It's not inconceivable that Jeane Dixon has similar
power.

But what of her apparent ability to spot a sick child though
even the child's doctor saw nothing wrong; to tell from looking at
a photo of a girl that she "was born with both hip sockets missing," although the girl's father, a doctor, hadn't discovered it; to
warn Ira Walsh to "see a doctor and prolong your life" although
he felt and looked fit aside from being overweight—and the advice was accurate—what of all that?

Stretching for an explanation that could deal with those facts
and yet discount any extrasensory ability, I could argue that what
she did was possible by normal means. In each case she may have
detected sensory clues to the illnesses or defects, perhaps even sub-
liminal clues: a remarkable achievement in itself.

And to represent the views of the die-hard skeptics: it is possible that Mrs. Dixon tells every overweight person she meets—
"See a doctor and prolong your life." And in the case of one in a
thousand she is right. This, of course, would mean there are possibly thousands of overweight people with identical advice from
Mrs. Dixon and by the law of probability some are bound to meet
and exchange notes—and then Mrs. Dixon's bubble would burst!
This may seem far out—but I want to give the skeptics a fair
hearing.

Her Critics

What do they say? She makes so many predictions, some must
come true. That she tells one person one thing and another the

opposite and then sends investigators only to the witness who heard the accurate prediction. That too many predictions are vague and could have many interpretations. That, after the event, she claims her prediction to have been more specific than it was in fact. That positive witnesses are close friends or in her employ. That many predictions are so far ahead that none of us will be alive to prove her right or wrong. That she has friends in high places and could get semi-secret information from them, then claim it came from an extrasensory source. That many predictions are projections of her own religious and political convictions. That she evades scientific investigation. That for a woman with a hotline to God she spends too much time and energy on commercial enterprises. That a sizable group of disillusioned former employees and friends say the idol has feet of clay.

Even conceding there's some or much truth in these criticisms, I think that the accumulation of evidence given by the witnesses in this book is so remarkable, that the skeptics must find other explanations than luck, faulty reporting, weak memories, inside information—to explain it away.

When I read a book about a psychic I wonder what has been left out to enhance the image of a faultless wonder worker, how much pressure has been put on the author to omit the negative and accentuate the miraculous.

I have tried to be fair—this side of libel—and hope that any witnesses prepared to talk whom I haven't reached will contact me to augment the record.

Jeane Dixon, being human, makes mistakes. She also rationalizes her mistakes, sometimes so effectively she almost convinces that her misses were near hits. Perhaps only masochists, saints, and pure mathematicians are scrupulous in recalling their failures as vividly as their triumphs.

A Challenge

The scientists are not easy to persuade. Dr. Louisa Rhine, for example, writes about people who make accurate predictions: "Informed guessing and likely suppositions cannot be ruled out, and vagueness of wording makes specific interpretation impossible.

Sometimes prognosticators . . . think that by depositing their utterances at some center like the Parapsychology Laboratory, they will establish its validity if the event comes to pass. They do not understand that validity cannot be established this way, but that it depends on the elimination of counter explanations."

I would like to give Dr. Louisa Rhine a friendly challenge. If, before the events, Jeane Dixon had told you the following, could you explain them collectively as other than evidence of ESP?

1. The United Nations secretary-general will be killed in a plane crash.

2. Supreme Court Justice Murphy will die within the next few days, although he is only fifty-six, appears to be in good health, and is planning to marry. (Not her precise words, but, I think, a fair paraphrase.)

3. Martha Rountree's house will burn to the ground within days.

4. The three astronauts will burn to death in a plugs-out-test at the end of the year.

5. Robert Kennedy is going to be fatally shot with two bullets in his head at the Ambassador Hotel.

6. Baroness Von Ammon will marry a man she has not yet met (nor have I, Jeane Dixon), with red hair and widely spaced teeth. The man she now loves is going to die. Her daughter will be killed or commit suicide.

7. President Kennedy will be killed within a week.

8. Proud Clarion is going to win the Kentucky Derby and will race in post position seven.

9. People will think someone close to Frank Sinatra is dead—then they'll discover he's all right.

Well, Dr. Rhine?

The battle between ESP skeptics and believers is almost at its peak. On one side is Dr. Louisa Rhine saying: "Precognitive experiences are probably nearly as common as acorns on oak trees." And on the other, mechanistic scientists hide behind their computers and say: "If you prove it to me, I still won't believe it!" They, too, are almost as common as acorns on oak trees. When pressed for a rational reply, these critics refute the evidence by accusing parapsychologists of faking the evidence or influencing it, perhaps unconsciously, to conform to the results they seek.

But while the skirmishing goes on, psychics like Jeane Dixon demonstrate outside the laboratory the practical application of ESP.

Knowing how any account of the supernatural or extrasensory can grow in the retelling, I thought it of value to have a record available, the testimony of mostly firsthand witnesses to Jeane Dixon's abilities.

If she is all she appears to be, and if, as some parapsychologists believe, all of us have such powers waiting to be unleashed, developed, and used—what does it signify?

For one thing, it calls for a new definition of man.

It challenges those who believe man's last breath on earth is his last activity of any kind—other than decomposing.

It refutes those who are sure man is just a bright machine, cowed by a stick, conned by a carrot; who ends his human existence as a handful of biodegradable chemicals.

It means that man does not have to be a prisoner of his senses, merely a talking animal with creative ideas, whose mind, confined to his brain, is doomed at death.

Man may well be an immortal spirit, not isolated from his fellow men by time, distance, or his own skin—and capable of "miracle" healings that baffle medical experts.

And Jeane Dixon points to these possibilities.

Appendix

Arthur Koestler, speaking before the annual convention of the Parapsychology Association in Edinburgh, Scotland, in September 1972, said:

In a recently published book [*The Challenge of Chance*] I tried to make the point that the unthinkable phenomena of parapsychology appear somewhat less preposterous in the light of the unthinkable proposition of modern quantum physics . . . Einstein, de Broglie and Schrödinger between them have dematerialized matter like the conjuror who makes the lady vanish from the box on the stage. Heisenberg replaced determinism by uncertainty and causality by statistics; Dirac postulated holes in space stuffed with electrons of negative mass; Thomson made a single particle go through two holes in a screen at the same time—which, Cyril Burt commented, is more than a ghost can do.

Photons of zero rest-mass have been observed in the process of giving virgin birth to twins endowed with solid rest-mass; Feynman made time flow backwards on his diagrams; and these are but a few glimpses from the surrealistic panorama which quantum physics has opened up to us. To paraphrase an old saying: Inside the atom is where things happen that don't. . . .

My purpose in reminding you of these well-known developments was to underline once more the fact that the mechanistic and deterministic world-view, which is still dominant in sociology, the behavioral sciences, and in the public at large, no longer has a leg to stand on; it has become a Victorian anachronism.

The nineteenth-century clockwork model of the universe is in shambles, and since matter itself has been dematerialized, materialism can no longer claim to be a scientific philosophy.

Bibliography

COMPILED BY DANIELLE BRIAN

American Society for Psychical Research, Journal of the.

Angoff, Allan (editor). *The Psychic Force.* Putnam, 1959.

Baird, Alex. *The Life of Richard Hodgson.* Psychic Press, 1949.

Bishop, Jim. *FDR's Last Year.* Morrow, 1974.

Carrington, Hereward, and Fodor, Nandor. *Haunted People.* Dutton, 1951.

Carter, Mary Ellen. *Edgar Cayce on Prophecy.* Paperback Library, 1968.

Christopher, Milbourne. *ESP, Seers & Psychics.* Crowell, 1970.

Cohen, Daniel. *Myths of the Space Age.* Dodd, 1965.

Crawford, W. J. *Experiments in Psychical Sciences.* Dutton, 1919.

Cummins, Geraldine. *Mind in Life and Death.* Aquarian Press, 1956.

Dingwall, E. J. *Some Human Oddities.* Home & van Thal, 1947.

Doyle, Arthur Conan. *The Edge of the Unknown.* Putnam, 1930.

————. *The History of Spiritualism*. Doran, 1926.

Dixon, Jeane, as told to Rene Noorbergen. *My Life and Prophecies*. Morrow, 1969.

Ebon, Martin. *They Knew the Unknown*. World, 1971.

Edmonds, Simeon. *Spiritualism—A Critical Survey*. Aquarian Press, 1966.

Ellenberger, Henri F. *The Discovery of the Unconscious*. Basic Bks., 1970.

Estabrooks, G. H. *Hypnotism*. Dutton, 1957.

Flournoy, Theodore. *The Letters of William James and Theodore Flournoy*. Univ. of Wis. Press, 1966.

Fodor, Nandor. *Between Two Worlds*. Parker Pub., 1964.

————. *Encyclopedia of Psychic Science*. Univ. Bks., 1966.

Ford, Arthur. *Known and Unknown*. Harper, 1968.

Forman, Henry James. *The Story of Prophecy*. Tudor, 1939.

Fuller, John G. *The Great Soul Trial*. Macmillan, 1969.

Gardner, Martin. *Fads and Fallacies in the Name of Science*. Dover, 1952.

Garrett, Eileen. *Many Voices*. Putnam, 1968.

————. *The Sense and Nonsense of Prophecy*. Farrar, Straus, 1950.

————. *Telepathy*. Berkley, 1968.

Hall, Trevor H. *The Spiritualists*. Duckworth, 1962.

————. *The Strange Case of Edmund Gurney*. London, 1964.

Hansel, C. E. M. *ESP: A Scientific Evaluation*. Scribner, 1966.

Heywood, Rosalind. *Beyond the Reach of Sense*. Dutton, 1961.

Hill, Douglass, and Williams, Pat. *The Supernatural*. Aldus, 1965.

Houdini, Harry. *Houdini the Magician—Enemy to Spirits*. Harper, 1924.

Huxley, Aldous. *The Doors of Perception and Heaven and Hell*. Harper, 1954.

James, William. *The Will to Believe . . . and Human Immortality*. Dover, 1956.

Jastrow, Joseph. *The Subconscious.* Houghton, 1906.

Koestler, Arthur. *The Roots of Coincidence.* Random House, 1972.

Lewinsohn, Richard. *Science, Prophecy and Prediction.* Harper, 1961.

Lodge, Sir Oliver. *Past Years.* Scribner, 1932.

——. *Raymond or Life and Death.* Doran, 1916.

Maudsley, Henri, M.D. *Natural Causes and Supernatural Seemings.* Library, 1930.

Montgomery, Ruth. *A Gift of Prophecy.* Morrow, 1965.

Murchison, Carl (editor). *The Case For and Against Psychical Belief.* Clark Univ., 1927.

Murphy, Gardner, and Ballou, Robert O. (editors). *William James on Psychical Research.* Viking, 1960.

Myers, F. W. H. *Human Personality and Its Survival of Bodily Death.* Univ. Bks., 1961.

Panati, Charles. *Supersenses.* Quadrangle Bks., 1974.

Parapsychology, Journal of.

Prince, Walter. *Noted Witnesses for Psychic Occurrences.* Boston Society for Psychic Research, 1928.

Rhine, J. B. *New Frontiers of the Mind.* Farrar, 1937.

—— (editor). *Progress in Parapsychology.* Parapsychology Press, 1971.

—— and Brier, Robert (editors). *Parapsychology Today.* Citadel Press, 1968.

Rhine, Louisa E. *ESP in Life and Lab. Tracing Hidden Channels.* Macmillan, 1967.

——. *PSI. What Is It?* Harper, 1975.

Rider, Fremont. *Are the Dead Alive?* Dodge, 1909.

Robbins, Ann Manning. *Past and Present With Mrs. Piper.* Holt, 1922.

Roberts, Estelle. *Fifty Years a Medium.* Jenkins, 1959.

Schmeidler, Gertrude (editor). *Extrasensory Perception.* Atherton, 1969.

Schwarz, Berthold, E., M.D. *A Psychiatrist Looks at ESP*. Signet, 1965.

Smith, Alson J. *The Psychic Source Book*. Creative Age, 1951.

Spraggett, Allen. *The Unexplained*. New Am. Lib., 1967.

Steinour, Harold. *Exploring the Unseen World*. Citadel Press, 1959.

Stone, W. C. Clement, and Browning, Norma Lee. *The Other Side of the Mind*. Prentice-Hall, 1964.

Tabori, Paul. *Harry Price*. Athenaeum Press, 1950.

———. *Companions of the Unseen*. Univ. Bks., 1968.

Theta.

Twigg, Ena. *Ena Twigg: Medium*. Hawthorn Bks., 1972.

Tyrell, G. N. M. *Science and Psychical Phenomena*. Society for Psychical Research, 1953.

Vasiliev, L. L. *Mysterious Phenomena of the Human Psyche*. Univ. Bks., 1965.

Warcollier, Rene. *Mind to Mind*. Creative Age, 1948.

Williams, Gertrude Marvin. *Priestess of the Occult*. Knopf, 1946.

Wolstenholme, G. E. W., and Millar, Elaine D. P. (editors), *Extrasensory Perception*. Citadel Press, 1969.